DAVID J BREEZE
WITH AN ESSAY BY GORDON DONALDSON

A QUEEN'S PROGRESS

AN INTRODUCTION TO THE BUILDINGS ASSOCIATED WITH MARY QUEEN OF SCOTS
IN THE CARE OF THE SECRETARY OF STATE FOR SCOTLAND

HISTORIC BUILDINGS AND MONUMENTS

Scottish Development Department

EDINBURGH
HER MAJESTY'S STATIONERY OFFICE

CONTENTS

Cover
Linlithgow Palace and St
Michael's Kirk from across
Linlithgow Loch, painted by
Robert M Greenlees RSW in
1856.

Inside Front Cover
Linlithgow Palace.

Opposite
The north tower of the Palace
of Holyroodhouse.

HMSO publications are available from:

HMSO Bookshops

13a Castle Street, Edinburgh, EH2 3AR   (031) 225 6333
49 High Holborn, London, WC1V 6HB   (01) 211 5656 (Counter service only)
258 Broad Street, Birmingham, B1 2HE   (021) 643 3757
Southey House, 33 Wine Street, Bristol, BS1 2BQ   (0272) 24306/24307
9–21 Princess Street, Manchester, M60 8AS   (061) 834 7201
80 Chichester Street, Belfast, BT1 4JY   (0232) 238451

HMSO Publications Centre
(Mail and telephone orders only)
PO Box 276, London, SW8 5DT
Telephone orders (01) 622 3316
General enquiries (01) 211 5656

HMSO's Accredited Agents
(see Yellow Pages)

And through good booksellers

Designed by D Adams
HMSO/GD

© Crown Copyright 1987
First published 1987

ISBN 0 11 493343 X

INTRODUCTION

Mary R

MANY BOOKS have been written about Mary Queen of Scots, but few have paid much attention to the buildings in which she lived. Those buildings which Mary visited in Scotland and which still survive are a tangible link with the queen who was executed on 8 February 1587. Over 24 of them are held in trust for the nation by the Secretary of State for Scotland and cared for on his behalf by Historic Buildings and Monuments, Scottish Development Department. Several more are owned privately, and, in most cases, are still inhabited. This book is not a life of Mary, but an account of her years in Scotland as seen through her connection with these buildings.

The range of buildings in the care of the nation extends from Linlithgow Palace, where Mary was born on 8 December 1542, through Stirling Castle, where she was crowned, Dumbarton Castle, whence she sailed for France, the Palace of Holyroodhouse, her principal home in Scotland, Edinburgh Castle, where her son, the future James VI and I, was born on 19 June 1566, to Dundrennan Abbey, where Mary spent her last night on Scottish soil on 15 May 1568. They include several of the castles and abbeys where Mary stayed during her royal progresses round Scotland between 1562 and 1566, and other buildings which she visited, such as Crichton Castle, where she attended the wedding of her half-brother in 1562. Crichton Castle was one of the strongholds of James Hepburn, Earl of Bothwell, later to be Mary's third husband.

The queen's relations with the great men of the time, often her kinsmen, are an integral part of her story. Many of the principal seats of these nobles are in the care of Historic Buildings and Monuments and are described in this book. They include Aberdour Castle, seat of James Douglas, Earl of Morton, Kinneil Palace, one of the several houses of James Hamilton, Duke of Châtelherault and Earl of Arran, and Dirleton Castle, stronghold of Patrick, Lord Ruthven, leader of the group which murdered David Riccio, the queen's secretary.

Many of these monuments already possess guide-books, outlining their history and describing the remains. This book is not intended to duplicate these publications, but to investigate the link between Mary and the individual buildings. More detailed treatment of these monuments can be found in the individual site guide-books.

This book begins with a survey of Mary's reign by Professor Gordon Donaldson, Historiographer Royal, and continues into an account of Mary's reign with the descriptions of the buildings arranged round its main episodes. The story is further enlivened by portraits of the main participants, photographs of furnishings, artefacts and coins, and maps. The maps indicate the extent of the journeys undertaken by Mary. The dates of her stay and the buildings visited during these journeys are given in heavy type in the captions.

The *Deuil Blanc*, or white mourning, portrait of Mary, after Clouet. The original was probably painted in 1559 when Mary was in mourning for her father-in-law, Henry II of France.

MARY'S LIFE AND REIGN

'She is a goodly personage, hath withall an alluring grace, a pretty Scottische accente, and a searching wit, clouded with myldness.'

Nicholas White to Sir William Cecil, February 1569

THE LIFE which ended at Fotheringhay Castle on 8 February 1587 has been described as containing both 'glorious tragedy' and 'modern history'. Romance, glamour, mystery and drama there were in plenty. Mary Stewart was Queen of Scots, Queen of France and, some thought, rightful Queen of England. She was three times married and three times widowed: her first husband, Francis II, King of France, died of an agonising illness at the age of only sixteen; the second, her first cousin, Lord Darnley, was murdered in Edinburgh when he was only twenty-one and the crime has provided a 'whodunit' which has intrigued investigators ever since; Mary's third marriage, to James Hepburn, Earl of Bothwell, lasted only a month, and after 11 years of captivity he died in a Danish prison when he was little over forty. Two men who wooed Mary—the French poet Châtelard and the English Duke of Norfolk—lost their heads in consequence, and a third—the Scottish Earl of Arran—lost his wits. A man who was accused of loving her—the Italian musician, David Riccio—was brutally murdered almost before her eyes at Holyrood. If fatality dogged Mary, it no less dogged those who associated with her.

Mary herself, Queen of Scots in 1542 at the age of one week, was in Scotland only from her birth until she was five and again from her nineteenth year until her twenty-sixth; between those two spells in Scotland she spent a dozen years in France, and the last 19 years of her life were passed as a prisoner in England. Only during the period of her active rule in Scotland from 1561 to 1567 did Mary have much voice in determining her movements, but in that period she was—as was then the way of sovereigns—much on the move, and she visited places as far apart as Aberdeen, Inverness, Inveraray, Dunoon, Dumfries and Jedburgh.

The vicissitudes of Mary's life were due only in small measure to her personal relationships, her great charm, her accomplishments, her fine presence and her political skill; nor were they due entirely to the folly and impulsiveness which she sometimes displayed. They were the consequence rather of political circumstances, national and international.

Scotland was a small and poor country on the fringe of the stage of European diplomacy, but there were situations in Queen Mary's time which gave her kingdom an importance almost ludicrously disproportionate to its population and resources. Scotland's role could hardly be other than that of a satellite, but the question was whether the country would be in the orbit of England, of France, or perhaps of Spain. In French eyes, Scotland was a base from which to threaten England in the rear, while England thought that her own security lay in bringing Scotland under her domination. This political situation was nothing new, for Scotland and France had been allies against England since the end of the thirteenth century. But the Reformation injected a new, religious, element into international relations. Luther's revolt had started in 1517, and by the 1530s parts of Germany, the Scandinavian countries and England had all broken with the papacy. It was evident that if the Pope could retain the allegiance of Scotland that would provide a stronghold for the Roman Catholic cause in the north, and for a generation Scotland was seen as a possible base from which a counter-reformation, headed by France or Spain, might recover England for Rome. On the other hand, a Protestant England was anxious to carry Scotland

Linlithgow Palace, birthplace of Mary Queen of Scots, viewed from across the loch in winter.

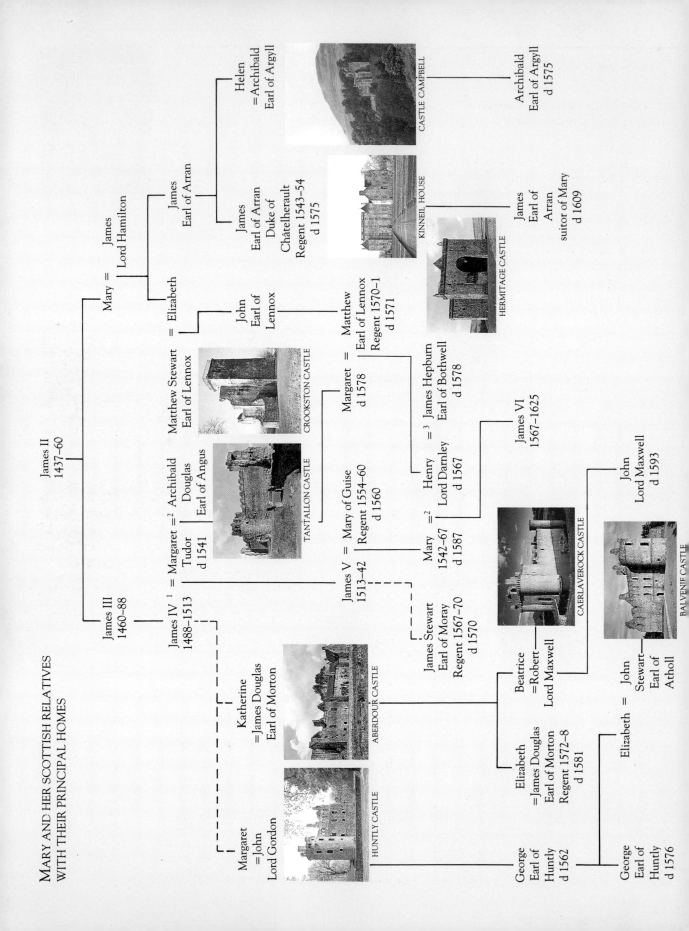

MARY AND HER SCOTTISH RELATIVES WITH THEIR PRINCIPAL HOMES

James II
1437–60

James III
1460–88

Mary = James Lord Hamilton

James Earl of Arran

Helen = Archibald Earl of Argyll

James Earl of Arran Duke of Châtelherault Regent 1543–54 d 1575

Archibald Earl of Argyll d 1575

CASTLE CAMPBELL

Elizabeth = John Earl of Lennox

Matthew Earl of Lennox Regent 1570–1 d 1571

James Earl of Arran suitor of Mary d 1609

KINNEIL HOUSE

HERMITAGE CASTLE

James IV ¹ = Margaret Tudor d 1541 =² Archibald Douglas Earl of Angus

Matthew Stewart Earl of Lennox

CROOKSTON CASTLE

Margaret d 1578

TANTALLON CASTLE

James V = Mary of Guise
1513–42   Regent 1554–60
           d 1560

Henry Lord Darnley d 1567

=³ James Hepburn Earl of Bothwell d 1578

Mary ²=
1542–67
d 1587

James VI
1567–1625

Katherine = James Douglas Earl of Morton

Margaret = John Lord Gordon

ABERDOUR CASTLE

James Stewart Earl of Moray Regent 1567–70 d 1570

Beatrice = Robert Lord Maxwell

Elizabeth = James Douglas Earl of Morton Regent 1572–8 d 1581

CAERLAVEROCK CASTLE

John Lord Maxwell d 1593

HUNTLY CASTLE

George Earl of Huntly d 1562

Elizabeth = John Stewart Earl of Atholl

George Earl of Huntly d 1576

BALVENIE CASTLE

with her and create a Protestant Great Britain as a counterpoise to the Roman Catholic powers on the continent.

Even before her birth Mary's fortunes had been closely bound up with the political and ecclesiastical rivalries of the great powers. Her father rejected suggestions that he should align himself with England and decided instead to take Scotland into the French and papal camp, hence his marriage to the Frenchwoman, Mary of Guise, who was the mother of Queen Mary. When Mary became Queen of Scots on her father's death in

1542, Henry VIII of England saw a dramatic opportunity to align Scotland with his realm, and it was agreed that the infant queen should marry Henry's son, Edward, afterwards Edward VI, a boy of five. But there was opposition from the pro-French and papal party in Scotland, and the Scots repudiated this agreement. Henry, in his fury, began a series of devastating invasions of Scotland which, as the English aim was to win Mary's hand for Edward, are known as The Rough Wooing. In 1547, after the Scots had been heavily defeated at Pinkie, English garrisons were planted at several places in south-east Scotland. Mary,

Edward VI, aged about five years, after Hans Holbein.

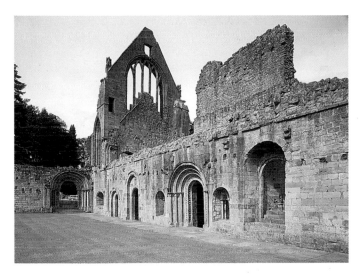

The four Border abbeys suffered grievously during the English invasions of the 1540s; in clockwise order—Dryburgh, Melrose, Jedburgh and Kelso.

Dunglass Collegiate Church in East Lothian was established by Sir Alexander Home in 1450. On 16 August 1544 an English raiding party from Berwick upon Tweed burned the village of Dunglass, but the church was held against them and in a sortie the Scots killed one Englishman and hurt two others.

A testoon of Mary minted in 1553 while she was in France.

had become queen in 1558, but as her mother, Anne Boleyn, had been married to Henry VIII in the lifetime of his first wife, Katharine of Aragon, Roman Catholics thought Elizabeth illegitimate and believed that the throne of England should go instead to Mary Stewart in right of her descent from Henry VII. Thus Elizabeth, rather than see a rival claimant to her throne established on England's northern frontier, intervened on behalf of the Scottish rebels. In July 1560 (after the death of Mary of Guise in June), it was agreed that both English and French forces should withdraw from Scotland, and in the following month a Scottish parliament abolished papal authority, adopted a Protestant Confession of Faith and forbade the celebration of Mass.

The successful insurgents, who had among them James Hamilton, Earl of Arran and (since 1549) Duke of Châtelherault, heir presumptive after Mary, and Lord James Stewart, Mary's half-brother, toyed with the idea of deposing their absent queen, but they were divided on the issue and some of them calculated that Mary, apparently with an assured future as Queen of France, might now not return to a Scotland which had rejected France and much that France stood for. However, after a reign of only a year and a half, Francis died in December 1560 and this, in effect,

who had been born in Linlithgow and had spent her childhood mainly there and at Stirling, was at this point sent for a few weeks to the greater safety of the island-priory of Inchmahome.

The Scots found that they could not eject the English occupying troops by their own resources and had to seek the help of their old allies the French. French help was given, but only on condition that Mary was sent to France. So in 1548 Mary, who had once been designated the bride of the heir to the throne of England, sailed from Dumbarton as the prospective bride of the heir to the throne of France. Scotland did not see her again for 13 years, and, while she was growing up in France, her mother was in 1554 appointed Regent of Scotland.

In 1558 Mary was married to the Dauphin, who next year became King Francis II of France, so that under 'Francis and Mary, King and Queen of France and Scotland' there was a 'union of the crowns' between the two countries, ruled as they were by the same sovereigns. Contemporaries in Scotland who were critical of the French connection, either because they valued the independence of their country or because they were attached to the cause of the reformers, feared that, under the descendants of Francis and Mary, Scotland would be absorbed into France. In 1559 a revolt broke out against the French-dominated administration.

The Scots, who a dozen years earlier had sought French help to eject the English, now sought English help to eject the French. Elizabeth Tudor

James Hamilton, Duke of Châtelherault and Earl of Arran, Regent of Scotland 1543–54. Châtelherault was only fifty-six when this portrait by Arnold Bronckhorst was painted.

threw Mary back on Scotland. She preferred to be queen regnant there rather than to play second fiddle as queen dowager in France; besides, she may have reasoned that a base in Scotland would improve her prospect of succeeding to the English throne after the elimination of Elizabeth either by natural causes or (which must have seemed equally likely) as a result of a successful revolt. So Mary left France in August 1561, made her way by sea to Leith and took up residence in the Palace of Holyroodhouse.

It was an indication of Mary's confidence in the loyalty of her subjects that she did not bring a French army with her, and her confidence was justified for a time as a result of the singularly wise policies which she pursued, in association with the Lord James (who became Earl of Moray in 1562) and William Maitland of Lethington, Secretary of State. Although Mary insisted on having Mass in her own chapel, she made no attempt to interfere with the reformed religion and indeed gave it official, legal and financial recognition, while she suppressed a rebellion by the Earl of Huntly, who might have headed a Roman Catholic reaction. An attempt was also made to reach an accommodation with Elizabeth, on the understanding that Elizabeth would be secure in England for life but that Mary would

The queen and her four Maries. This tableau of costume figures, by Anne Carrick and MacDonald Scott, is on view in Smailholm Tower, near Kelso.

have the right of succession. Elizabeth refused to agree to such terms and plans for a meeting of the two queens came to nothing.

For nearly four years after her return to Scotland Mary had considerable success. Many thought her policies eminently fair and she gained support through her attractive personality. Mary had few near kinsfolk in Scotland, at least of lawful birth, though she was related in one way or another to several of the earls, including Arran, Argyll, Huntly, Lennox and Morton. She was somewhat isolated in Scottish society, but seems to have made friends readily with men and women who were not in the highest social strata and she had cordial relations with many devoted servants. Her 'Four Maries' (Beaton, Fleming, Livingston and Seton) involved her with their families on a peculiarly intimate level. Apart from the subjects whom Mary met on social terms, she met, or at least saw, a great many of her people on her progresses through the country. In those days there were two practical reasons why a sovereign should move about: a lot of food, owing to the royal household, could more easily be consumed where it was raised than transported to some centre; and when there was no running water conditions in any residence became intolerable after a time and the obvious solution was to move on and allow the premises to be cleaned. But there was a third reason, one of policy: when there was little throughout the country to remind people of the central government, it was important that a sovereign should allow herself to be seen by as many as possible of her subjects and give them the chance to say 'God bless that sweet face'. Each

James Stewart, Earl of Moray, half-brother to Mary.

MARY AND HER FOREIGN RELATIVES

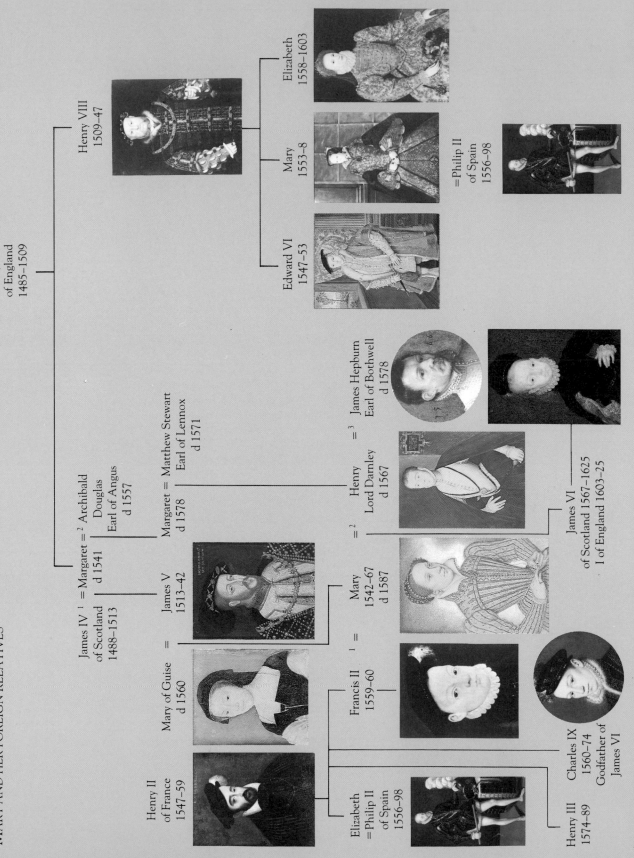

Henry VII
of England
1485–1509

Henry VIII
1509–47

Edward VI
1547–53

Mary
1553–8

=Philip II
of Spain
1556–98

Elizabeth
1558–1603

James IV ¹ =Margaret= ² Archibald
of Scotland   d 1541   Douglas
1488–1513   Earl of Angus
                               d 1557

Margaret = Matthew Stewart
d 1578   Earl of Lennox
           d 1571

Henry   = ³ James Hepburn
Lord Darnley   Earl of Bothwell
d 1567   d 1578

= ²

James VI
of Scotland 1567–1625
I of England 1603–25

James V   =
1513–42

Mary
1542–67
d 1587

Mary of Guise
d 1560

¹ =

Francis II
1559–60

Henry II
of France
1547–59

Elizabeth
=Philip II of Spain
1556–98

Charles IX
1560–74
Godfather of
James VI

Henry III
1574–89

Don Carlos, son of Philip II of Spain.

Robert Dudley, Earl of Leicester, painted by an unknown artist in about 1575.

year from 1562 to 1566 Mary was in Fife in the spring. In 1562 and 1564 she was in Aberdeen and Inverness in the summer. She was in Argyll and Ayrshire in the summer of 1563 and in the autumn of 1565 and 1566 she was in the south-west and south. Her tall, athletic figure was seen hunting and golfing.

Successful though Mary was in the first years after her return to Scotland, no settlement could be lasting which did not take account of a second marriage, as it was inconceivable that she should remain unmarried and equally inconceivable that her husband should be a mere consort: he would be king and would at least share in the shaping of policy. Suits were advanced, with varying degrees of optimism, on the parts of half-a-dozen European kings and princes, but the most serious negotiations were for a match with Don Carlos, son and heir of Philip II of Spain. There was nothing unrealistic about that, for Philip himself had lately been the husband of Elizabeth's predecessor, Mary Tudor. But Spain was the most strongly papalist of powers, and Protestants viewed with alarm the prospect of a marriage which would have put Scotland firmly into the counter-reformation camp and terminated the tolerant policy which Mary was pursuing in Scotland. John Knox, the minister of Edinburgh, lectured the queen mercilessly on the perils of the Spanish match and (according to his own account) told her plainly that subjects had a right to be heard in such matters. Queen Elizabeth was an interested party in Mary's matrimonial prospects, if only because Mary's husband might well be the progenitor of future sovereigns of England. She was ready enough to negative proposals by others, but when asked to make a positive suggestion, the only offer she could make was the incredible one of Robert Dudley, Earl of Leicester, 'that shop-soiled and notorious widower' whose own relations with Elizabeth were thought by some to be improper.

Don Carlos meantime had become insane, and when Mary found that Elizabeth would not recognise her rights in the English succession and had no better candidate than Leicester, she was free to turn her attention elsewhere. She fell in love with her first cousin, Henry, Lord Darnley, and married him in July 1565. Darnley's mother stood next to Mary in the English succession and, as he had been born and brought up in England, some thought he had a better right than Mary. But, apart from in a sense strengthening Mary's claim to England, the marriage was a disaster. It alienated Elizabeth, who saw danger in this union of two claimants to her throne; although Darnley was not a Roman Catholic, the fact that the marriage was by Roman Catholic rites alarmed the Protestants; and nobles who had hitherto been in Mary's counsels saw themselves displaced by a feather-brained youth who, as King Henry, shared sovereignty with his wife. A rebellion was raised by Châtelherault and Moray (who hoped in vain

Aerial view of **Berwick upon Tweed** looking south. The fortifications of this Border town were rebuilt by Elizabeth I of England as defence against the Scots between 1558 and 1569, when building ceased although the work was not finished. The surviving ramparts are among the best artillery defences in Europe. The walls of Berwick were a defence against France in a sense, for construction started during the regency of Mary of Guise, when the French were gaining the ascendancy in Scotland, and ended shortly after the exile of Mary Queen of Scots and the establishment of a pro-English Protestant government north of the border. Mary Queen of Scots viewed Berwick from nearby Halidon Hill in **November 1566** during her progress through south-east Scotland.

for English help), but it was suppressed by a campaign in which Mary took an active part.

It did not take Mary herself long to see that the Darnley marriage had been a mistake, but she did little to recover the confidence of her subjects. It did her no good in the eyes of the Protestant ministers or of her nobles that she seemed to give too much of her time to an Italian musician, David Riccio, and her husband suspected—or professed to suspect—that Mary's personal relations with Riccio were not above reproach. The outcome, on 9 March 1566, was the brutal seizure of Riccio from the queen's supper table at Holyrood and his murder almost before her eyes; Mary herself, six months pregnant, was roughly treated, and the conspirators may have intended that their crime would endanger the lives of Mary and of her unborn infant. She survived, and detached Darnley from his fellow-conspirators, who were banished. A prince, the future James VI, was born in Edinburgh Castle on 19 June 1566 and received Roman Catholic baptism in December.

The number of Darnley's enemies was mounting. The lords who had rebelled on the occasion of his marriage were pardoned, but nothing had happened to diminish their initial hostility. The assassins of Riccio, who had fled to England, hated Darnley for abandoning them, and the permission given to them to return in December 1566 almost amounted to Darnley's death-warrant. Darnley preferred his pleasures to state business in which he should have played a part, and Mary found him not only intellectually worthless but morally despicable. It seems doubtful if there was any cordiality between the couple after the summer of 1566, and Mary's alienation from her husband seemed to be accompanied by a growing partiality for James Hepburn, Earl of Bothwell. Those who were attached to Mary for either personal or political reasons began to consider how she might be released from an intolerable union and seem to have consulted her about possible plans.

There can be no doubt about Mary's knowledge that Darnley's life was in danger from more than one quarter, but it is far from certain that she was a party to the plot which led to his murder on 10 February 1567, when the house in which he was living at Edinburgh was blown up and his body, dead by strangling or smothering, was found

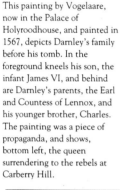

This painting by Vogelaare, now in the Palace of Holyroodhouse, and painted in 1567, depicts Darnley's family before his tomb. In the foreground kneels his son, the infant James VI, and behind are Darnley's parents, the Earl and Countess of Lennox, and his younger brother, Charles. The painting was a piece of propaganda, and shows, bottom left, the queen surrendering to the rebels at Carberry Hill.

James Hepburn, Earl of Bothwell, third husband of Mary Queen of Scots.

Jean Gordon, daughter of the 4th Earl of Huntly and Bothwell's first wife.

Elizabeth I of England, painted by or after G Gower, about the time of the execution of Mary.

in the adjoining garden. Much remains mysterious about the crime, but suspicion soon fell on Bothwell and on Mary as his accomplice. The case against them looked even blacker when Bothwell divorced his wife and married the queen on 15 May 1567. A rebellion was raised against the supposedly guilty pair, and two armies confronted each other at Carberry on 15 June, but the army of Mary and Bothwell showed little heart for the fight and after Bothwell got safely off the field Mary surrendered, to be taken to Edinburgh in disgrace. The proclaimed aim of the rebels had been to 'liberate' Mary from Bothwell, but she was at once hustled off to captivity in Lochleven Castle and on 24 July was compelled to abdicate in favour of her son, who became James VI at the age of thirteen months. The Earl of Moray was appointed Regent.

Mary's imprisonment in Lochleven lasted nearly a year. She was then at liberty for 11 days, but in that space of time thousands of men flocked to her standard, moved by loyalty to their lawful sovereign, approval of Mary's policies, affection for her and sympathy for her misfortunes. However, on 13 May she was defeated at Langside. She fled to the south-west, crossed the Solway and appealed to Queen Elizabeth.

Mary's unexpected arrival in England presented an embarrassing problem. It would not have been in her own interest to allow or encourage her simply to return in the way she had come and risk capture and renewed imprisonment or worse. What she wanted was England's help to recover her throne, but Elizabeth could hardly work to overthrow a Scottish régime, that of Moray, which was Protestant and anglophile, in favour of one that might prove less reliable. At the same time, to allow Mary to remain in England at all, and certainly with freedom of action, meant the existence of a focus for discontent with Elizabeth and for Roman Catholic plots. The solution, arrived at slowly, was to make no formal judgement on Mary's guilt, no formal decision on the differences between her and Moray and no sentence against her, but to keep her in England under restraint, yet with a household and state befitting a queen. During 19 years she was moved around—Bolton Castle, Tutbury Castle, Sheffield Castle, Wingfield Manor, Chatsworth, Buxton, Chartley and Fotheringhay. While she had recreation in hunting as long as her health allowed, and a pastime in embroidery, it was a weary life, enlivened by obsessive plotting which in the end brought upon her sentence of death for being a party to plans for the assassination of Elizabeth.

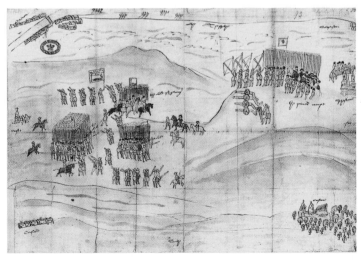

A contemporary sketch of the scene at Carberry Hill on 15 June 1567. The queen's army lies to the right and that of the rebel lords to the left. Bothwell, on horseback, sits behind the cannon, while the queen is led across to the opposing army.

15

BIRTH

'As goodly a child as I have seen . . . and as like to live.'

Sir Ralph Sadler, English ambassador, March 1543

MARY STEWART was born at Linlithgow Palace on 8 December 1542. She never saw her father who died six days later at Falkland Palace, broken, it is said, by the defeat of his army by the English at the battle of Solway Moss. Thus Mary was Queen of Scots from the first week of her life.

Although Linlithgow Palace is now a bare shell, devoid of roofs, windows, floors and furnishings, most of its structure is little different from that within which the infant queen spent the first seven months of her life. The main change has been to the north wing. On 6 September 1607 the whole range crashed to the ground, and it was rebuilt for James VI ten years later, between 1618 and 1620, as the dates on it proclaim.

At Linlithgow Palace the queen's apartments appear to have been placed above the king's. Today none of the floors of the queen's apartments remains. The site of the queen's bed-chamber, where Mary would have been born, however, survives, floorless and roofless above the king's bed-chamber in the north-west tower. Above this bed-chamber is Queen Margaret's bower, said to be the favourite room of Margaret Tudor, Mary's grandmother.

At the time of Mary's birth, Linlithgow Palace was one of the principal royal residences of Scotland. There had been a royal residence on the site for over 300 years, since the time of David I (1124–53). In 1425 James I commenced rebuilding

Linlithgow Palace from the north. Mary would have been born in the queen's bedroom, which probably lay in the north-west corner (to the right, in shadow). She lived here from **8 December 1542 until 27 July 1543**.

The marriage of Mary's parents, James V of Scotland and Mary of Guise, was blessed here, in St Andrews Cathedral, on 11 June 1538; the couple had previously been married by proxy in France. The first two children of the marriage, both sons, were to die before the birth of Mary four years later.

Top
Linlithgow Palace from the outer court. The five tall windows light the chapel. The windows of the king's suite, to the left, would have looked out over the gardens.

the old manor destroyed by fire in the previous year. His successors extended the building which, with the exception of the reconstruction of the north wing in 1618–20, reached its most complete state under James V. The palace now consisted of four ranges round a square courtyard with a tower at each corner. Beyond lay the outer close. Its entry from the town, the outer entry, was built by James V.

Linlithgow Palace was particularly favoured by the queens of Scotland. The future James V was born here and his mother, Margaret Tudor, was widowed whilst in residence. Mary of Guise declared it to be the most princely home she had looked upon. The infant Mary Queen of Scots lived at Linlithgow with her mother, Mary of Guise, for the first seven months of her life.

On 1 July 1543 agreement was reached with England for the marriage of Mary to Edward, Prince of Wales, the son and heir of Henry VIII of England. The Scots, fearing that Mary might be abducted south in preparation for her eventual marriage, moved the baby to Stirling later that month. Mary was not to return to Linlithgow Palace for nearly 20 years.

The room above the king's bed-chamber at **Linlithgow Palace,** with the four-paned window, was probably the queen's bed-chamber.

Linlithgow Palace and St Michael's Church from the air.

The outer entry, built about 1535. The panels over the entrance record the Orders of Knighthood to which James V belonged—the Garter of England, the Thistle of Scotland, the Fleece of the Empire and St Michael of France. The originals were replaced by copies in the last century.

The insignia of the Orders of the Garter (left) and Thistle (right) on the outer entry.

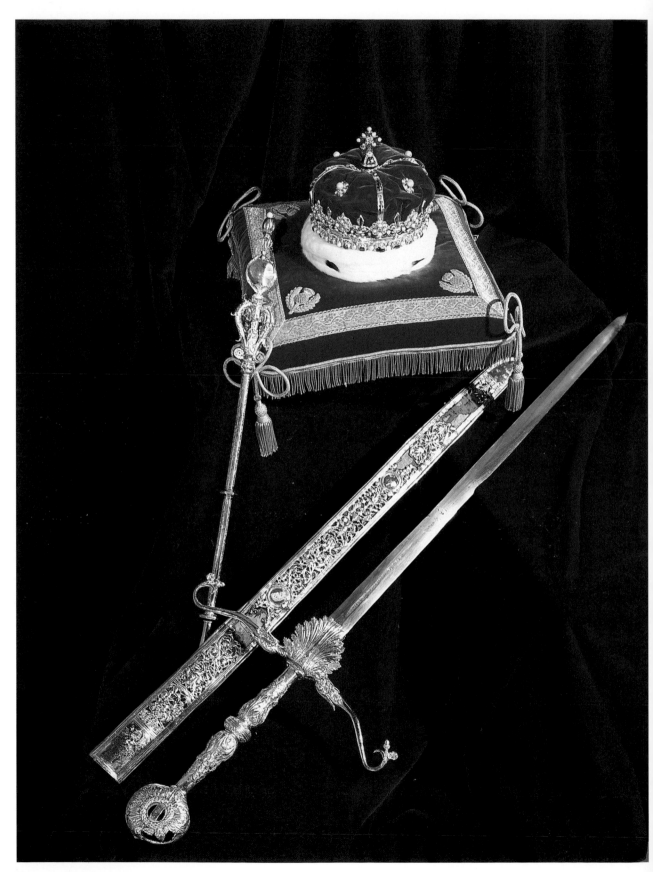

CORONATION

'The olde Quene and the yong Quene, by common assent of all parties, are this day removed to Sterlyng.'

Sir Ralph Sadler, English ambassador, to Henry VIII, 27 July 1543

ON 27 JULY 1543 the infant queen was brought to Stirling Castle, which was to be her home for the next four and a half years. This castle was a place of considerable strength and Mary would have been safe from all but a major invasion. She was placed in the care of Lord Erskine, whose family had a kind of hereditary right to protect the heir to the throne. It was in the chapel of Stirling Castle that Mary was crowned Queen of Scots on 9 September 1543 when she was nine months old.

James IV had built a chapel in Stirling Castle about 1501, and this would have been where Mary was crowned. It seems probable that the present Chapel Royal is merely an adaption and remodelling of James IV's chapel by James VI, who carried out the work in preparation for the christening of his son and heir, Prince Henry, in 1594. The other buildings in the upper square were also in existence at the time of Mary's coronation: the King's Old Building, probably built as a lodging for James IV; the great hall built by James IV about 1500; and the palace erected by James V in the 1540s.

Mary would have lived in the palace. Built by her father between 1540 and 1542, and only just completed before his untimely death, this was one of the first buildings in Britain to have been constructed in the Renaissance style. This was no doubt the result of the strong French influence in Scotland following the successive marriages of James V to two French princesses. The delightful

Stirling Castle sits on an extinct volcano, its slopes scarped by glaciers. In the Middle Ages the castle's position at a strategic communications centre enhanced its importance. Mary lived at Stirling from **27 July 1543 until February 1548,** apart from the three weeks when she was taken to Inchmahome Priory.

The crown, sceptre and sword used at the coronation of Mary. James IV was presented with the sceptre by Pope Alexander VI in 1494 and the sword by Pope Julius II in 1507. James V remodelled the sceptre and in 1540 made, probably rather than refashioned, the crown. Thus the coronation of Mary Queen of Scots was the first time that the new crown had been used. This is the oldest crown in the British Regalia.

The east façade of the palace, behind which lie the king's bed-chamber (right) and the queen's bed-chamber (left).

This figure of James V, the builder of the palace, still adorns the north-east corner 450 years later.

and ornamental exterior is now in marked contrast to the largely bare interior. Like Linlithgow, at the time of Mary's stay, the walls would have been covered in tapestries. Now these and all the furniture have gone. All that survives are the fine, sturdy fireplaces and the timber roundels, known as the Stirling Heads, which formerly adorned one of the ceilings of the king's apartments.

Mary's upbringing was in the hands of her guardian, Lord Erskine. Henry VIII tried to limit the influence on the young queen of her mother by forbidding Mary of Guise to live in the castle. In view of the fact that she had a French mother it is surprising that Mary was not taught French but had to learn it when she arrived in France.

During these years relations between Scotland and England declined catastrophically. Henry VIII used military means to try to enforce his will on the Scots. The English harried the Borders and on 10 September 1547 defeated the Scots army at Pinkie near Musselburgh. During this invasion Mary was moved for safety from Stirling Castle to the priory on the island of Inchmahome in the Lake of Menteith. This was an obvious choice, for Lord Erskine's son, Robert, was the commendator, or lay administrator, of the priory; Robert was not at Inchmahome at the time for he fought in the Scots army at Pinkie, where he was killed. Mary and her mother stayed on the island for less than three weeks, returning to Stirling once the danger had received.

The fireplace in the queen's outer hall.

A detail of the south façade of the palace.

The queen's outer hall, which now provides a home for most of the Stirling Heads.

A jester depicted on one of the Stirling Heads.

The Chapel Royal. The date, 1594, over the door, refers to the remodelling of the chapel by James VI for the christening of his eldest son, Henry. The original building had been created nearly a century earlier by James IV, grandfather of Mary Queen of Scots.

Inchmahome Priory looking across the cloister garden to the chapter-house. In the foreground is the cellar of the guest house and the prior's lodging, where Mary may have stayed. The priory was established in the thirteenth century and most of the buildings date to this time. Mary stayed here for three weeks in **September 1547**.

Dumbarton Castle was drawn by Captain John Slezer about 1690. This view shows the south-western front facing the Clyde, as it might have been in Mary's time. The medieval gatehouse was swept away during extensive modifications in 1735. Dumbarton was a royal castle and in the early 1540s was held by Matthew, Earl of Lennox, Mary's future father-in-law. He was succeeded as governor by Châtelherault, who was required to surrender the castle to Mary in April 1562. Lennox briefly regained his governorship in 1564–5 when he returned to Scotland after an exile of 20 years. Mary was here from **22 February to July 1548**; she returned to Dumbarton Castle in 1563, staying there on **14** and from **17 to 19 July 1563** while on her tour of western Scotland.

Departure for France

'The princes past to France to be brocht up under the feir of God.'

Diurnal of Occurrents in Scotland

HENRY VIII'S martial policy had the reverse effect from that intended, for far from forcing the Scots to come to terms with the marriage of their queen to Edward, Prince of Wales, it drove them towards an alliance with France. In the months after the disastrous defeat at Pinkie, negotiations were commenced with the French and in July 1548 these came to a head when the Scots Parliament gave its approval to the marriage of Mary and the son and heir to Henry II of France, the four-year-old Dauphin Francis. In return, a French army, 6000 strong, arrived to help the Scots.

On 22 February 1548 Mary moved to Dumbarton Castle on the Clyde, a more inaccessible place to English armies. In July French galleys came to take her to France. Henry II sent his own royal ship to carry the young queen, and on 7 August, after waiting several days for favourable winds, Mary and her court sailed down the Clyde, from there taking a course southwards towards France.

Mary was not accompanied by her mother, but she did take two of her half-brothers, her guardian Lord Erskine, her governess and aunt Lady Fleming, and her four maids of honour—the four Maries— Mary Beaton, Mary Fleming, Mary Livingston and Mary Seton.

Dumbarton Castle today, seen from across the Clyde. In the centre sits the Governor's House, built in 1735, with, behind, the guard house, visible on the Slezer drawing.

St Andrews Castle was the seat of the Archbishop of St Andrews, Cardinal Beaton, the leader of the Roman Catholic and pro-French party in Scotland. Here in March 1546 Beaton burned to death the Protestant reformer, George Wishart. Three months later the castle was besieged by the Protestants and Beaton was himself killed and his body hung from the wall-head.

Following its seizure by Beaton's murderers, St Andrews Castle was besieged by government forces. During the siege, which lasted a year, a mine was dug from beyond the castle ditch towards the fore tower by a party of French sappers. However, the defenders retaliated and commenced excavating a counter-mine from immediately in front of the fore tower and succeeded in breaking into the mine and stopping further work. The castle fell in 1547 and the defenders, who included John Knox, were sent to the galleys, where they worked as galley-slaves for the next two years.

FRANCE

'As her youth grew on, we saw her great beauty and her great virtues grow likewise.'

Pierre Brantôme

MARY AND HER PARTY landed at Roscoff on the French coast on 13 August 1548. France was to be her home for the next 12 years. It is not the purpose of this guide-book to consider in detail Mary's homes outside Scotland, but some comment on her years in France is necessary.

As she was betrothed to the Dauphin Francis, Mary was taken into the French court and educated with the children of Henry II. For some years she shared a room with Elizabeth, the eldest of the royal sisters. Mary learned to speak French, which became her natural language of communication, Latin and Greek, Italian and Spanish. She was taught the social graces—dancing, singing and playing musical instruments. Drawing and needle-work formed part of her education. As she grew older she also came to enjoy hunting.

The French court travelled round the various royal palaces during the year in the same manner and for the same reasons as the Scottish court. Saint-Germain, Fontainebleau, Blois and Chambord were all regularly visited. The court was frequently received at Anet, the palace of Henry II's mistress, Diane de Poitiers.

Mary of Guise came to visit her daughter in France just once, in September 1550, staying for a year. Mary, however, had other close relatives in France. Her grandmother, Antoinette, Duchess of Guise, was able to keep a motherly eye on the young queen. Her uncles included Francis, Duke

The arms of Francis on the ceiling of the outer chamber of the queen's suite in the **Palace of Holyroodhouse**. The *fleur-de-lis* are quartered with the dolphin, Francis' symbol as Dauphin of France.

Opposite
The new wing of the palace at **Blois**, built between 1515 and 1524 by Francis I of France.

The royal palace at **Chambord**, built in the 1520s by Francis I of France.

of Guise, a famous soldier and, in 1558, captor of Calais from the English, and Charles, Cardinal of Lorraine. The Guise family were among the most powerful in France, and were looking forward to acquiring even more power when their niece became Queen of France. Her Guise relatives took a close interest in Mary's upbringing and a strong attachment grew up. Mary frequently stayed at the Guise houses, especially the palace of Joinville.

On Sunday 24 April 1558 Mary was married to the Dauphin Francis at a magnificent ceremony in front of the cathedral of Notre Dame in Paris. This open-air ceremony, was attended by many of the French nobility, led by the King and Queen of France, and was witnessed by a vast throng. Mary was fifteen and her husband fourteen.

Later that year another event occurred which was to have significant consequences for Mary: her cousin, Mary Tudor, Queen of England, died and was succeeded by her half-sister, Elizabeth. The new queen was a Protestant, and, in the eyes of Roman Catholics, illegitimate. Thus Mary was now, in the view of Roman Catholics, the rightful Queen of England. She announced this by quartering the arms of England with her own, but she made no other move to make good her claim.

Mary's marriage was followed a year later by that of her sister-in-law, Elizabeth, with Philip II of Spain. During a tournament which accompanied these festivities, King Henry II was mortally wounded and died ten days later. Mary was now, suddenly and in totally unexpected circumstances, Queen of France. The new King of France was a weak boy of fifteen; the real power rested in the hands of Mary's relatives, the Guises. But while Mary had finally realised her family's hopes, their—and her—triumph was to be shortlived.

During the months that Mary was Queen of France the seeds of future conflicts were being sown in Scotland. The Protestants were gaining in strength while the French troops and administrators were increasingly disliked by the Scots. After a painful illness, Mary of Guise died of dropsy on 11 June 1560 and in August the Reformation was proclaimed by the Scottish Parliament.

In November 1560 Francis too fell ill and in spite of careful nursing by Mary and his mother, died on 5 December; Mary had been Queen of France for less than 18 months.

Mary now had to decide her future. She might stay in France, where she was assured of a position as queen dowager, or return to Scotland; by March 1561 she had decided on the latter course. After making a tour of her Guise relatives, she sailed from France on 14 August, arriving at Leith only five days later. Mary was now eighteen.

A ducat of Mary and Francis minted in 1558. The arms on the reverse are of Francis Dauphin of France and King of Scots (left) and Mary Queen of Scots (right). Reproduced at about twice actual size.

Mons Meg, the great bombard manufactured in the 1440s and now in Edinburgh Castle, fired a salute to mark the marriage of Mary and Francis in 1558.

The tall tower house of Broughty Castle was built in the 1490s; the surrounding walls largely date to the remodelling of the castle in 1860–1 as a coastal fort to protect shipping on the Tay. The castle was captured by the English in September 1547 during the War of Rough Wooing, and remained in their hands for three years before being taken by Regent Arran. It was then garrisoned by French troops until 1559. The Treaty of Edinburgh in the following year provided for the withdrawal from Scotland of all but a token French force.

The west front of the **Palace of Holyroodhouse.** The nearer tower was erected by James V between 1529 and 1536, but the main front and the far tower were the work of Charles II's architect, Sir William Bruce, who commenced the remodelling of the palace in 1671.

THE PALACE OF HOLYROODHOUSE

'Fires of joy were set forth at night, and a company of most honest men with instruments of music, and with musicians, gave their salutations at her chamber window.'

John Knox, History of the Reformation

ON THE AFTERNOON of Tuesday 19 August 1561 Mary Queen of Scots took up residence in the Palace of Holyroodhouse in Edinburgh. This was to be her principal home for the next six years. The palace formed part of the great royal abbey complex at Holyrood which had been established on this site by King David I in 1128. Succeeding kings of Scots had frequently enjoyed the hospitality of the abbey by making the abbey's guest house their residence when in Edinburgh. James IV had constructed new ranges of rooms for his own use, and between 1529 and 1536 Mary's father, James V, further augmented these with additional buildings on an even grander scale. The original proposal was to form a new courtyard by placing a handsome wing, flanked by a tower at each end, to act as a façade to the additions already made by James IV. James V's plan was never completed. The north-west tower was built, and survives largely unaltered to this day, but his central range was replaced in 1676 when Charles II remodelled the palace and completed the original intention by the construction of the south-west tower.

The crown and thistle on the ceiling of the inner chamber.

The church of the abbey of Holyrood. The royal palace of Holyroodhouse grew out of the abbey.

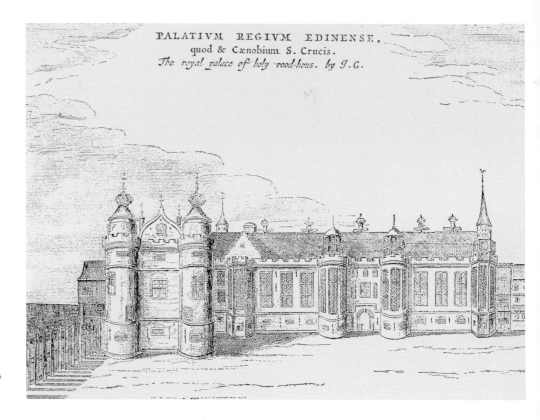

PALATIVM REGIVM EDINENSE,
quod & Cænobium S. Crucis.
The royal palace of holy rood-hous. by J.G.

The main front of the **Palace of Holyroodhouse**, drawn by John Gordon of Rothiemay about 1647. The palace in this view was little altered from that in Mary's time.

Part of the ceiling in the queen's outer chamber. The heraldry depicted on the wooden panels commemorates the close connections between the Scottish and French royal families. Shown here are the initials of James V, Mary of Guise and Henry II of France, while the arms towards the bottom left are of Mary of Guise.

In James V's new Palace of Holyroodhouse the queen's apartments were placed above the king's in the new tower, as at Linlithgow, but unlike Stirling where they were spread across the same floor of the palace with separate entrances but adjoining bedrooms. The king's rooms at Holyrood lay on the first floor, with the queen's on the second. When Mary came to live at Holyrood, she occupied these second-floor rooms, and the king's suite seems to have been used only during the brief periods that her second husband, Darnley, and her third, Bothwell, lived at the palace.

The queen's apartments consisted of two main rooms and two smaller rooms (see plan on page 58). The first room in the sequence was the outer chamber. This was entered from the stair tower in the north-east corner turret; there were in fact two stairs, the main, or great, turnpike and a smaller stair placed in the wall itself. In the outer chamber, Mary would have received ambassadors and other important visitors and perhaps have held formal dinners. Grand state occasions would probably have taken place in the adjoining rooms of the west range built by James V.

The inner chamber would have contained the queen's bed. This would have been a four-poster bed, surrounded by curtains which would have been drawn at night for privacy. A small stair connected this room to the king's bed-chamber on the floor below. Mary probably also used the inner chamber as a private living room, where she would have received those who were close to her, and where she possibly conducted less formal meetings with her nobles and officers of state. Before the queen's marriage to Darnley, Mary Fleming also slept in this room. Her bed, like most beds of the time, would have been put away during the day, to be brought out each night. Many members of the household simply slept where they could find a space, in a wall recess or on top of a trunk, elsewhere in the palace.

Two small rooms or closets opened off the inner chamber. These were Mary's most private rooms, the only rooms in the palace where she could escape from public attention. One of the closets probably contained the royal chamber box (of all Mary's palaces only Falkland contained a water closet). The north closet seems to have been

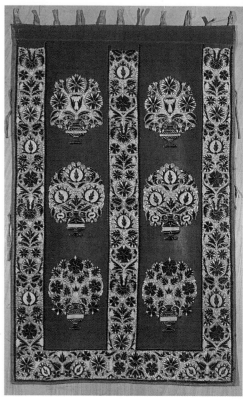

Pomander, to hold sweet smelling herbs, believed to have belonged to Mary Queen of Scots and preserved at the Palace of Holyroodhouse.

This woollen hanging, with applied black silk, embroidered with golden yellow silk, is said to have come from Lochleven Castle. The hanging is not the work of the queen, but of a professional needleworker. It may have served as a cloth of state, the hanging which denoted the royal presence in a room and which would have been placed behind the throne.

Part of a tapestry of the time of Mary Queen of Scots, now on display in Scone Palace.

A cabinet, said to have belonged to Mary Queen of Scots and preserved for many years by the Hepburn of Smeaton family. It is now in the Royal Museum of Scotland, Queen Street, Edinburgh.

regularly used as a dining room for small supper parties of Mary and her immediate entourage. Here also Mary's officers and counsellors may have attended her. This room was only 4 m (12 feet) square. On the evening of the murder of Riccio it contained a table, chairs and a day-bed.

The rooms in her Palace of Holyroodhouse must have seemed small to Mary after the spacious French palaces to which she was accustomed. The royal furnishings had suffered during the regencies of the Duke of Châtelherault and Mary of Guise, but the queen brought many new items with her. These included the canopies and hangings for 20 beds, tapestries, cushions and linen. Satin and velvet were used in some of the hangings and cushions. Mary brought with her from France two professional embroiderers and three upholsterers. They repaired the older furnishings and also made new bed hangings for the members of the queen's household.

The main state rooms used by Mary and her court were swept away in the rebuilding of Charles II. Here lay the Chapel Royal where Mary married Darnley and the great hall where she wed Bothwell. Mary's library probably also lay in this part of the palace. It included books in Latin, Greek, French, Italian, Scots and English and ranged over a variety of subjects: history and geography, poetry and prose, religion and music. Music was an important relaxation for Mary, and several of her household played or sang. An even greater passion was dancing. Mary might stay up after midnight dancing, and she also played cards into the early hours. Billiards, backgammon, chess and dice were other games played by the queen. Like all noble ladies she also embroidered, though none of her needlework dating from her years in Scotland survives.

The garden provided for outdoor relaxation and exercise. Gordon of Rothiemay's plan of Holyrood, drawn in 1647, shows formal gardens to north and south of the palace, and the existence of at least certain of these at the time of Mary is indicated by the English spy's sketch of 1544 which shows the northern gardens; it seems probable that James V was responsible for these.

Holyrood Park provided ample opportunities for archery, and probably hunting, but for Mary's great loves, hunting and hawking, she usually went further afield, perhaps to one of her other palaces.

John Knox, a leading Protestant reformer, who had several discussions with Mary at Holyrood.

Gordon of Rothiemay's plan of the palace and its grounds was drawn in 1647. It reveals the complexity of the palace; most of these buildings were swept away in the reconstruction of the 1670s. Around the palace lie the formal gardens, where Mary would have frequently taken her exercise. This plan shows that Mary's own rooms formed a tiny part of the whole palace complex.

Sketch plan of the **Palace of Holyroodhouse**, drawn in 1544 by an English spy.

THE QUEEN AND HER PALACES

'Decored with a Kingis palice, a beautiful temple and a pleasant loch.'

Bishop John Leslie, The Historie of Scotland

MARY POSSESSED four palaces in addition to Holyroodhouse: Edinburgh; Linlithgow; Stirling; and Falkland; while the guest house at Dunfermline was effectively used as a royal residence. Edinburgh, Linlithgow and Stirling were placed about a day's journey apart to the south of the Forth. Dunfermline lay just across the water in Fife, while Falkland lay in the heart of that county.

Edinburgh and Stirling Castles were initially strongholds; although sumptuous residences had been formed within them by James IV and James V. Certainly Holyroodhouse and Linlithgow pos-

sessed a defensive capability, but this was against casual attackers. They would have been little use against a determined foe. Falkland, far removed from the centres of power, was more a hunting palace, sited for the chase not war. Here Mary could hunt deer and wild boar in the Forest of Falkland, and indulge in another of her favourite sports, hawking.

All medieval monarchs, as we have seen, spent a considerable time on the move between their palaces and Mary was no exception. She spent a month at Stirling in summer 1562 and most of September, October and November there the

The gatehouse of **Falkland Palace,** built for James V.

Opposite
The Chapel Royal at **Falkland Palace,** built in the early sixteenth century and carefully restored over the last 100 years.

Dunfermline Abbey in Fife was founded by Queen Margaret, wife of Malcolm III, in the late eleventh century, but owed its great wealth and prestige to benefactions by David I in the 1120s. As at the abbey of Holyrood in Edinburgh, the guest house came to be frequently used by successive kings of Scots. Mary stayed here on several occasions while travelling through her kingdom; from **7 to 9** and again from **17 to 18 September 1565** with her new husband, Darnley. The building was given to Anne of Denmark, queen of James VI, by her husband on their marriage, and at this time it was completely rebuilt. Charles I, son of James and Anne, was born in Dunfermline Palace in 1600. In this view the abbey church rises above the palace, which is seen from across Pittencrieff Glen.

Falkland Palace in Fife was substantially modified by James V between 1537 and 1542 when this façade was added to the south range. The south front (right) is a magnificent illustration of the impact of French Renaissance ideas in Scotland at this time, and the gatehouse (left) bears a striking resemblance to the contemporary tower at the Palace of Holyroodhouse. The work was supervised by Sir James Hamilton of Finnart, a kinsman of the king. Sir James, who was executed for treason in 1540, probably influenced the design. It was at Falkland Palace that James V himself was to die only two years later.

following year. She was there again through April and May 1565 and in September and December 1566 when her son was lodged there. Falkland was sometimes used as a base for local travelling, though she stayed for much shorter periods. Linlithgow generally was used for single nights when travelling between Edinburgh and Stirling, and Dunfermline was similarly used when she was in Fife.

Edinburgh Castle served another function: it was the strongroom of the kingdom. Here were normally housed the crown jewels and the national records. Mary also had a library in the castle, which was broken up during her exile.

The Crown also possessed several castles throughout the kingdom. These royal castles included Blackness on the Forth, Doune north of Stirling, Inverlochy at the southern end of the Great Glen, Lochmaben near Dumfries, and Rothesay in the Firth of Clyde.

The tennis court at **Falkland Palace**, where 'real' or royal tennis was played.

The King's Knot, the great formal garden below **Stirling Castle**. The garden is thought to date to the time of Mary's grandson, Charles I, but her father, James V, employed a French gardener at Stirling in the 1530s and thus the establishment of a garden here may date to these years.

The royal palace in **Stirling Castle** seen across Queen Anne's garden.

Doune Castle was a royal castle. It had been built in the late fourteenth century by Robert Stewart, Duke of Albany, virtual ruler of Scotland from 1388 until his death in 1420. In 1527 the castle passed back into the hands of his family when his descendant, Sir James Stewart of Beath, was made keeper of the castle. His son, James, Lord Doune, was implicated in the murder of Riccio. Following Mary's flight to England, Lord Doune was suspected of being a supporter of the queen and was commanded to surrender the castle. It eventually surrendered to the Regent Lennox in 1570 after a siege of three days.

This view of **Linlithgow Palace** about 1678 by John Slezer shows the terraced gardens stretching to the west. There was formerly a wooden balcony overlooking the gardens.

...desty, and also of great
...and her matters.'

...France, 31 December 1560

Mary's Chancellor, whom she inherited
...her mother, was George Gordon, 4th Earl of
...ly. Huntly was Mary's own first cousin, being
...on of an illegitimate daughter of James IV.
...s Douglas, 4th Earl of Morton, and another
... cousin of Mary, succeeded Huntly as
...ncellor in 1562 and held the post more or less
...tinuously until becoming Regent for the young
James VI in 1572. Mary's Secretary of State was
William Maitland of Lethington, who married
another cousin, Mary Fleming, one of the four
Maries, in 1567.

Moray ...
eclipsed only briefly by Mary's husba...
and Bothwell.

Moray was a member of Mary's Privy Council, but
otherwise held no formal position in her govern-

George, 5th Lord Seton, one
of the masters of Mary's
household. The brother of
Mary Seton, one of the four
Maries, Lord Seton was a
consistent supporter of the
queen.

Opposite
Castle Campbell was the
lowland seat of Archibald
Campbell, Earl of Argyll, a
prominent member of the
Privy Council. Before it was
acquired by the Campbells, it
was known as Castle Gloom.
The tower house to the right
was built in the fifteenth
century, the ranges to the left
being added over the next two
centuries. Mary was here from
9 to 12 January 1563
attending the wedding of
Argyll's sister to James
Stewart, Lord Doune. The
festivities included banquets
and masques; one of these
included people dressed as
shepherds playing lutes. Two
years later the Earl of Argyll
joined the rebellion against
Mary and Darnley following
their marriage. In September
1565 the queen and the new
king passed close to Castle
Campbell during their
campaign against the rebels
and received the surrender of
the castle (see map on page
55).

Seton Collegiate Church, built
by the Seton family in about
1434 and extended by
successive generations, lay
beside their great house, which
was replaced by Robert Adam's
mansion in 1789.

The tomb (left) of John Maitland, 1st Lord Maitland and younger brother of Mary's Secretary of State, in St Mary's Church, Haddington. Maitland was a supporter of Mary in the years following her flight to England. The monument to the right is to his son, John, 1st Earl of Lauderdale, and his wife.

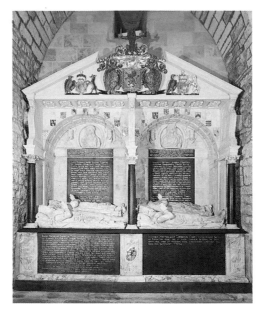

Lennoxlove, now the seat of the Duke of Hamilton, was formerly known as Lethington; it was the home of Secretary Lethington.

The four Maries formed part of the queen's own household. This included ladies of the bedchamber, maids of honour, equerries, valets and secretaries. Not all the queen's household were Scots. David Riccio, who entered the queen's service as a valet and rose to be secretary of French correspondence, was an Italian. Mary's chamberlain was French, as was her fool, Jardinière, and her apothecary.

The queen's officers and councillors were members of the noble families of Scotland. The power of these families was securely based on landed estates and the people who lived on their land and provided their lords with a substantial following. The power base of the Lennoxes lay in the Glasgow area, the Hamiltons in middle Clydesdale and across central Scotland, the Hepburns in East Lothian and the Borders, and the Gordons in north-east Scotland.

Kinneil House was built in the 1550s by James Hamilton, Duke of Châtelherault and Mary's heir until the birth of her son, James, in 1566. The house consisted of two separate buildings—the tower house to the left and the palace to the right. The wing on the right contains wall paintings dating to the time of its construction about 1553. In 1569 the tower house was blown up by the Earl of Morton. It was rebuilt in the 1670s, when the two parts of the house were joined by the pavilions at the sides of the tower house.

The arms of James Hamilton, Duke of Châtelherault, in the Arbour Room of Kinneil House.

The younger sons of the nobility often took Holy Orders. In this way the power of Scots lords could be extended, and younger sons provided for without dividing the heir's patrimony. One brother of the Duke of Châtelherault was Archbishop of St Andrews from 1549 to 1571, while another was Bishop of Argyll; one son was Commendator of Arbroath Abbey and another Commendator of Paisley Abbey. Another Hamilton was Abbot of Kilwinning in Ayrshire. The south transept of Kilwinning Abbey Church, seen here above the cloisters and the entrance to the chapter-house, still stands to full height.

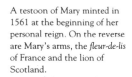

A testoon of Mary minted in 1561 at the beginning of her personal reign. On the reverse are Mary's arms, the *fleur-de-lis* of France and the lion of Scotland.

Aberdour Castle in Fife was one of the seats of James Douglas, Earl of Morton. Morton probably built the range to the left, while one of his successors, William Douglas, 7th Earl of Morton, erected the eastern range to the right in the first half of the seventeenth century.

James Douglas, 4th Earl of Morton, was one of Mary's Privy Council and became her Chancellor in 1562. Morton was involved in the murders of Riccio and of Darnley, and was one of the leaders of the rebellion against Mary and Bothwell. At Carberry he was one of the commanders of the rebel cavalry. Morton was Regent for James VI from 1572 to 1578. He was executed in 1581 for his part in the murder of Darnley. This portrait has been attributed to Arnold Bronckhorst, a Flemish painter who came to Scotland about 1578.

Noltland Castle, on the island of Westray, Orkney, was built by Gilbert Balfour, one of the masters of the queen's household. Gilbert was involved in the murder of Cardinal Beaton in 1546, was besieged in St Andrews Castle, and subsequently served in the galleys. He and his brother, Sir James Balfour, helped in the murder of Darnley, while his wife was sister to Adam Bothwell, Bishop of Orkney, who married Mary and Bothwell. Gilbert was active in preventing Bothwell from securing a base in Orkney following the queen's surrender to the rebels at Carberry Hill in 1567. In 1571 and 1572 Gilbert was active on Mary's behalf on the mainland and was present at Blackness Castle when it was held by the Hamiltons on behalf of the queen. After the capture of the castle he fled from Scotland and died in Sweden in 1576. He probably built Noltland Castle as a bolt-hole to retire to in times of trouble, hence its array of gun-loops.

44

MARY AND HUNTLY

'In all these broils I assure you I never saw her merrier, never dismayed.'

Thomas Randolph, English ambassador, to Sir William Cecil,
Spynie, 18 September 1562

MARY RULED most of Scotland through the agency of her nobles and officials. It was important, however, that she should occasionally remind these men that she was their queen. This could be done by summoning them to court, where they attended upon her, and by travelling through her kingdom to make her presence felt, just as her father and grandfather had done. One of Mary's most important royal progresses took place in 1562. In that year she travelled as far north as Inverness, in a journey which took over three months to complete.

The main purpose of this particular progress was to curb the power of the Earl of Huntly, who ruled the north-east of Scotland virtually with a free hand. The earl was head of the Gordon family and held several important castles and estates in his own right or from the Crown. His family ties extended his power even further, while he was also a possible leader of the Roman Catholic cause in the country. Moreover, from 1546 until his death in 1562 he was Chancellor of Scotland. His open display of wealth had caused the French ambassador to recommend to Mary of Guise, who had visited Huntly Castle in 1556, to 'clip his wings'. Now her daughter proceeded north with that intention.

Mary left Holyrood in early August and passed westwards, staying at Linlithgow Palace on 12 August, then at Stirling Castle. She crossed the Forth about 19 August, and proceeded in a

Opposite and above
Huntly Castle, centre of power of the Gordon family. George, 4th Earl of Huntly, rebuilt the palace following his visit to France with Mary of Guise in 1550; it was completed in time for the visit of Mary of Guise in 1556. His grandson, the 1st Marquis of Huntly, added the splendid series of oriels which are surmounted by an inscribed frieze.

Mary stayed here at **Glamis Castle**, seat of Lord Glamis, on **22 August 1562** on her journey north. The castle dates to the fifteenth century, but it was remodelled on the French château style by the 3rd Earl of Strathmore between 1650 and 1695.

Map indicating the route taken by Mary Queen of Scots and her entourage in 1562.

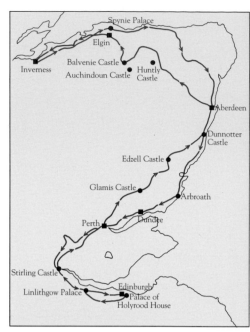

Mary spent the nights of **23 and 24 August 1562** at **Edzell Castle**. The tower house, built by the Lindsays of Glenesk, was erected only a few decades before Mary's visit. The gardens in the foreground were laid out in 1604 by Sir David Lindsay, Lord Edzell. A meeting of the Privy Council was held here on **25 August** during Mary's stay. It was attended by the Earls of Mar, Marischal and Morton and William Maitland of Lethington.

Dunnottar Castle sheltered Mary on the night of **26 August 1562,** and again between **5 and 7 November 1562.** This castle, built in the fourteenth century but considerably extended later, was the seat of the Earl Marischal. The queen returned to Dunnottar in **September 1564.**

Balvenie Castle was the seat of John Stewart, 4th Earl of Atholl, son-in-law of the Earl of Huntly, but a staunch supporter of the queen during her reign and exile. John Stewart built the lodging to the east side of the courtyard (right in this view) between 1547 and 1557. Mary probably stayed in this building during her visit on **4 and 5 September 1562.**

Spynie Palace was the official residence of the Bishops of Moray. Mary stayed here from **17 to 19 September 1562** mustering her forces while returning from Inverness to Aberdeen. By a strange quirk of fortune, her host was Bishop Patrick Hepburn, a relative of the Earl of Bothwell whom Mary was later to marry. The earl had spent part of his childhood at Spynie and returned in 1567 while fleeing from defeat at Carberry. The great tower at Spynie, one of the largest in Scotland, was built by Bishop David Stewart in the fifteenth century, and modified by Bishop Patrick Hepburn, bishop from 1538 to 1573. The palace was taken into the care of the State in 1973 and work is still proceeding on its fabric. Thus the palace can be viewed only from the outside.

north-easterly direction towards Aberdeen. She spent some days here visiting the university and holding court. The next move was to Inverness, and Mary's party was harried *en route* by Sir John Gordon, one of Huntly's sons. Thus, suspecting a trap, Mary refused an invitation to stay at Huntly Castle, but pressed on to Darnaway Castle, which formed part of the domain of her half-brother, Lord James Stewart, newly-created Earl of Moray. Arriving at Inverness, Mary was refused entry by its keeper, another of Huntly's sons. This was treason as Inverness was a royal castle, not a Huntly property. However, the earl himself was more sensible and issued orders that Mary be admitted.

Mary stayed but a few days in Inverness, where she was enchanted by the wild Highlanders, before returning to Aberdeen. Now matters came to a head. Huntly was out-manoeuvred by the queen and her advisers and, rather than throw himself on the queen's mercy, he offered battle. At Corrichie, 20 km (12 miles) west of Aberdeen, his troops were defeated by Moray, and Huntly himself fell off his horse, dying probably of a heart attack.

Mary now showed magnanimity in her triumph. She contented herself with executing Huntly's son, Sir John Gordon, and confiscating the contents of Huntly Castle. Huntly's eldest son was spared, but he did not win royal favour again until 1565. Mary stayed at Aberdeen until mid November, when she returned to Edinburgh.

The body of George Gordon, 4th Earl of Huntly, was brought home to be buried in the family tomb here in Elgin Cathedral in April 1566. Huntly, found guilty of treason following his death at Corrichie, was at first buried in the Blackfriars Church in Edinburgh. The reversal of his attainder for his son enabled his family to reclaim his body and give it a decent burial

Auchindoun Castle was the stronghold of 'Edom O'Gordon', brother to the Earl of Huntly. In October 1562 Mary demanded, and received, the keys to the castle. The central tower, clearly visible in this view, is said to have been built by Thomas Cochrane, favourite of James III.

Glenluce Abbey was founded in 1192 by Roland, Lord of Galloway, for the Cistercian Order of monks. It was visited by Robert the Bruce and by James IV. Mary stayed here on the night of **9 August 1563.** In this view the abbey church rises above the claustral buildings.

MARY'S PROGRESSES

'Her grace lodged in a merchant's house; her train were very few.'

Thomas Randolph, English ambassador, to Queen Elizabeth, 5 February 1565

ARY'S TOURS round Scotland continued throughout her reign. Between February and May 1563 she was in Fife, in July and August in the west and south-west. This was one of her longest progresses. She journeyed first to Glasgow and from there to Hamilton, to the home of her cousin, James Hamilton, Duke of Châtelherault. She then turned north-westwards, moving along the north side of the Clyde, via the royal castle of Dumbarton, to Inveraray, seat of the Earl of Argyll, another cousin, and also her brother-in-law. From Inveraray she returned via Toward to the south side of the Clyde and continued southwards to Glenluce Abbey, following, for the last leg of this part of the journey, the pilgrim's way over the moor (now part of the Southern Upland Way), passing the Laggangairn standing stones, now in State care. Like several of her ancestors, including her father and grandfather, she visited Whithorn Cathedral-Priory, the oldest ecclesiastical site in Scotland. From Dumfries she returned northwards to Edinburgh.

1564 saw another long journey, this time to Inverness. From Stirling Mary took the route of

The bridge across the Forth at Stirling, built between 1410 and 1415, was frequently used by Mary.

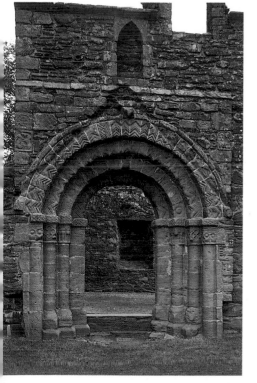

Whithorn is the oldest Christian place in Scotland. It was reputedly founded by St Ninian in the fifth century. A cathedral-priory for Premonstratensian canons-regular was built here in the twelfth century. Little survives today above ground apart from the nave of this cathedral, which also served as the priory church. The nave, seen here from the south, was altered on several occasions both before and after the Reformation of 1560. Mary stayed here on the night of **10 August 1563.**

49

Map showing the route of the royal progress in 1563.

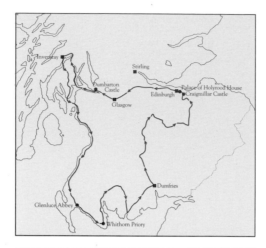

the modern A9 northwards, but her return journey was by way of Aberdeen. In October 1565 she made a ten-day trip as far as Dumfries, but otherwise in that year, the year of her marriage, she travelled no further from Edinburgh than Glasgow, Dunkeld and St Andrews.

The latter part of 1566, following the birth of her son, saw another important journey, now indelibly intertwined with the name of Bothwell. Through October and November she was in the south-east of Scotland, travelling out to Jedburgh, and thence to Hermitage, and returning down the Tweed and along the coast.

The whole apparatus of royal government accompanied Mary on these travels. In 1562 her half-brother, Lord James Stewart, Earl of Moray, her Secretary of State, William Maitland of Lethington, and other members of her Privy Council such as the Earl of Argyll, formed part of the royal party. The English ambassador, Thomas Randolph, was also present and a letter he wrote from Spynie Palace to Elizabeth's chief minister, William Cecil, still survives.

Meetings of the Privy Council were sometimes held in the castles and monasteries in which the court stayed. On 25 August 1562 a Council was held at Edzell Castle on the journey north to Aberdeen, while Councils were held at Dumfries, Glasgow, Perth, St Andrews and Stirling and in Jedburgh four times in October and November 1566. Mary also often held justice ayres (assizes) while visiting the different parts of her kingdom.

Tantallon Castle in East Lothian, principal stronghold of the Red Douglases, Earls of Angus. The castle dates from the fourteenth century, but was modified on several occasions through the following centuries. Tantallon was garrisoned by royal forces until 1565 when it was handed over to James Douglas, Earl of Morton, guardian of his young nephew, Archibald, 8th Earl of Angus, and effective head of the Douglas family during his nephew's minority. Mary visited Tantallon Castle on **19 November 1566.**

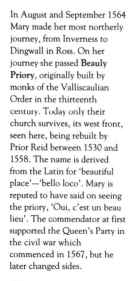

In August and September 1564 Mary made her most northerly journey, from Inverness to Dingwall in Ross. On her journey she passed **Beauly Priory**, originally built by monks of the Valliscaulian Order in the thirteenth century. Today only their church survives, its west front, seen here, being rebuilt by Prior Reid between 1530 and 1558. The name is derived from the Latin for 'beautiful place'—'bello loco'. Mary is reputed to have said on seeing the priory, 'Oui, c'est un beau lieu'. The commendator at first supported the Queen's Party in the civil war which commenced in 1567, but he later changed sides.

The royal party would be of considerable size. In addition to the queen, several members of her Privy Council and her household, there was usually a body of soldiers for protection. State papers were required so that government could continue, clothes for the queen and her attendants and furniture for the houses and palaces where the royal party stayed. These buildings would contain a number of trestle tables, forms (collapsable benches), and timber beds. Walls would be bare, usually plastered, occasionally wood-panelled. Tapestries, bed hangings and linen, the throne canopy and hangings, collapsable chairs, cushions and many other items would have travelled with the court. Oak chests (called kists) would have carried eating and drinking utensils, clothes or state papers. Grass or rushes were used to cover the floors as carpets were virtually unknown in Scotland at this time.

Mary usually travelled on horse-back, as did her attendants and bodyguard. Carts would frequently have been used to transport the heavier and bulkier items. While journeying between Edinburgh and Linlithgow in December 1565 the pregnant queen was carried in a litter. Coaches were rare at this time: Mary of Guise introduced the first coach to Scotland. The passage across the Firth of Forth at Queensferry and over the Firths of Clyde and Tay would have been by ship, while rowing boats were used on Loch Leven. Mary's final journey from Scotland on 16 May 1568 was by fishing boat.

The queen frequently stayed at monasteries as she travelled round Scotland. This is because, although no longer functioning in a religious sense, the members of the community still lived on the premises and retained part of their revenues, and thus could offer reasonable accommodation to the royal party. On **11 November 1562** Mary is known to have stayed in **Arbroath** and it seems probable that she stayed here in the abbot's house. This building dates to the fifteenth and sixteenth centuries, and it remained in use for a variety of purposes until this century. The commendator at the time of Mary's visit was Lord John Hamilton, a loyal supporter of the queen during the civil war which lasted from 1567 to 1573.

Blair Castle, one of the seats of the Earl of Atholl. In **August 1564,** when Mary stayed here on her return from Inverness, a special hunt was arranged. 3000 Highlanders drove 2000 deer from the surrounding hills into the glen for the hunt, during which 360 deer and 5 wolves were killed.

Far left
Mary had dinner at **Balmerino Abbey** on **28 January 1565** while travelling between Edinburgh and St Andrews. This view shows the east end of the chapter-house, which was remodelled in the sixteenth century.

Henrie Stewart Duke of
Albanye and, Marie
Quem of Scotland
1566

52

MARY AND DARNLEY

'Her Majesty took well with him, and said that he was the lustiest and best proportioned long man that she had seen . . . well instructed from his youth in all honest and comely exercises.'

Sir James Melville, Scots ambassador to England, Memoirs

I T WAS THE DUTY of a monarch to marry and beget a successor. This was no less the duty of a queen than a king. Mary's cousin, Mary Tudor, had married Philip II of Spain and the question of whom Elizabeth should marry now that she was queen was an important matter for her advisers; some years were to pass before the unusual decision of Elizabeth not to marry became apparent.

There was no need for Mary to hurry. When she returned to Scotland she was still only eighteen. Nevertheless, the question was of significance for Scotland from the moment of Francis' death. Various foreign suitors were advanced—French, Spanish, Swedish, and English—and Scots. In February 1565, however, Mary's eighteen-year-old cousin, Henry, Lord Darnley, travelled to Scotland from England, where he had lived since birth. He and Mary met for the first time in several years on 17 February in Fife.

Mary soon fell in love with this handsome young man, and on Sunday 29 July 1565 they were married in the Chapel Royal in the Palace of Holyroodhouse (this was not the abbey church, which survives, but another chapel swept away in the rebuilding programme of Charles II). The bridegroom was proclaimed Henry King of Scots. There followed three or four days of festivities: dancing and feasting, enlivened by masques.

The marriage was not received everywhere in Scotland with such rejoicing. Darnley was carried away by his new position, and became overbearing and haughty. Mary's half-brother, the Earl of Moray, with her cousin and heir, the Duke of Châtelherault, were driven into opposition and, after an abortive rebellion, fled to England. Darnley was left as the first man of the kingdom.

Crookston Castle was one of the three major properties of the Lennox family. It was named after its founder, Robert Croc, a vassal of Walter the Steward, in the twelfth century, and acquired by the Lennoxes in the fourteenth century, when this tower was built. One of its famous owners was Sir John Stewart, constable of the Scots fighting in France. Crookston was abandoned by the Lennoxes in the sixteenth century in favour of their new palace at Inchinnan. Crookston Castle was given by James VI to his cousin and was retained by that branch of the family until 1673.

Henry, Lord Darnley, was seventeen when this painting was executed.

Opposite
Mary and Darnley, depicted as Queen and King of Scots, in the sixteenth-century *Seton Armorial*.

The arms of Mary Queen of Scots and Henry King of Scots in the Chapel Royal at **Falkland Palace**.

Mary and Darnley spent the weeks following their marriage—their honeymoon—dealing with the opposition of the Earl of Moray, the Duke of Châtelherault and their allies. Mary had no trouble in gaining sufficient support throughout the kingdom to force her half-brother, Moray, to flee to England. On **14 October 1565** the queen and king attended a banquet at **Lochmaben Castle**, seen here, and the next day they set off back to Edinburgh.

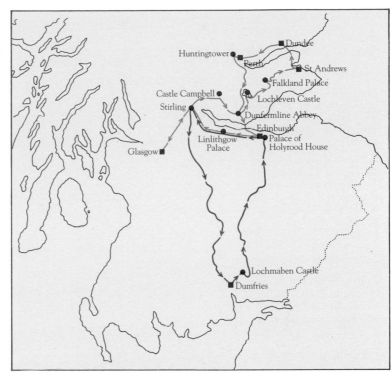

Route taken by Mary and Darnley in their campaign against the rebels, the 'Chaseabout Raid'. In September 1565 they operated north of the Forth, moving south on 8 October to chase the rebels out of the country.

Sir William Bruce of Earlshall supported Mary's marriage to Darnley in 1565. Mary is reputed to have visited his house (above) built only 20 years before in 1546.

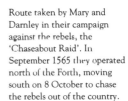

A ryal of Mary and Henry minted in 1566. The reverse bears the royal coat of arms.

A painting of 1838 showing
the queen's bed-chamber, as it
then was, with the tapestry
pulled aside to show the little
room where Riccio was seized
and the entrance to the
staircase used by the
murderers. All the furniture
and the tapestries date to at
least a century after the time
of Mary. The bed is more
elaborate than that which
Mary would have used. The
main difference lies in the
ornamental top, which is
distinctive of the late
seventeenth century.

THE MURDER OF RICCIO

'Lord Ruthven . . . with his complices . . . most cruelly took him forth of our cabinet, and at the entry of our chamber give him fifty-six strokes with . . . swords.'

Mary to the Archbishop of Glasgow, 2 April 1566

THE CLOUDS of infatuation soon fell from Mary's eyes and her love for her new husband turned to dislike. Darnley, in his frustration, struck out at Mary's friends. He signed a bond with several Scottish lords, including the Earls of Argyll, Morton and Moray and Lord Ruthven, to further his cause. On 9 March the conspirators struck, murdering the queen's confidant, David Riccio, in Mary's own rooms in Holyroodhouse.

David Riccio was an Italian aged about thirty-five who had come to Scotland in 1561. Three years later he was appointed the queen's secretary for French correspondence. Mary was charmed by Riccio's musical abilities, especially his playing of the lute, and he became her confidant. The power which this position gave him in turn brought him the hatred of the Scottish nobles, who considered him a low-born upstart. Riccio's friendship with Darnley only served to increase this hatred. As Darnley's relations with Mary deteriorated, he began to see Riccio as the cause of the rupture. Riccio thus attracted the enmity of several powerful people and this was his downfall.

On the evening of Saturday 9 March 1566 Mary was having supper with five of her household in the north closet, in her apartment on the second floor of the great tower in the Palace of Holyroodhouse. The queen was now six months pregnant with the future James VI. Darnley

The Palace of Holyroodhouse.

Dirleton Castle in East Lothian, one of the properties of Lord Ruthven. It was built in the thirteenth century by the de Vaux family and passed from them to the Halyburtons and subsequently to the Ruthvens. All three families modified and extended the castle. The great round tower in the foreground was erected by the de Vaux family, but the Halyburtons were responsible for the adjacent entrance (the bridge is a modern replacement of the original). In March 1566, after Riccio's murder, Dirleton was surrendered to one of Mary's officers and remained in royal hands for the following year.

A plan of the queen's suite of rooms at **Holyroodhouse**.

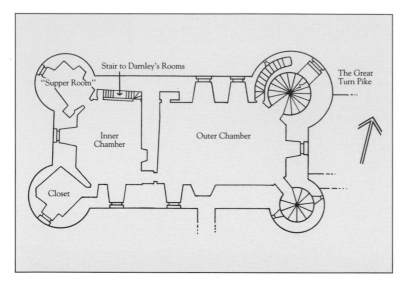

"Supper Room"

Stair to Darnley's Rooms

The Great Turn Pike

Inner Chamber

Outer Chamber

Closet

entered the room from the stair leading up from his own apartments on the floor below, followed by Lord Ruthven and several of his men. In spite of Mary's protestations, Riccio was dragged out to the head of the main staircase in the outer chamber and stabbed to death. The conspirators were now in possession of the queen's palace and several of Mary's supporters had to flee for their lives.

On the following day Mary worked on her husband and brought him round to her side and on the Monday they escaped from Holyroodhouse, riding for five hours to Dunbar Castle. Here Mary rallied her forces and only a week later was able to return to Edinburgh in triumph. Morton, Ruthven and their followers fled to England, where Ruthven died in June.

This depiction of the murder of Riccio was painted by Sir William Allan (1782–1850). Patrick, Lord Ruthven, is the figure in armour.

The Ruthvens were established at **Huntingtower** as early as the twelfth century, and retained the castle until 1600 when all their estates were forfeited and the name of the castle changed from the Place of Ruthven to Huntingtower. Mary was here from **25 to 27 June 1565** and again from **16 to 17 September 1565** while on honeymoon with Darnley. The windows were inserted into the medieval fabric of the castle in the seventeenth century.

The painted wooden ceiling of the hall on the first floor of the eastern tower at **Huntingtower**, dating to about 1540.

THE BIRTH OF PRINCE JAMES

'Immediately upon the birth of the Prince, all the artillery of the castle was discharged, and the lords, the nobles, and the people gathered in St Giles Church to thank God for the honour of having an heir to their kingdom.'

Claude Nau, History of Mary Stewart

I N APRIL 1566 Mary was persuaded by her Council to move into the royal lodging in Edinburgh Castle in preparation for the birth of her child. The lying-in-state began on 3 June and a baby prince was born on 19 June. The birth of an heir to the throne was an important occasion and it was welcomed by the lighting of bonfires and by a service of thanksgiving in St Giles Church in Edinburgh. The new prince was not only heir to the throne of Scotland, but, by virtue of his Tudor blood, might have hopes for eventual succession to the throne of England.

It took Mary some time to recover from the birth of her son and she did not leave the castle until 28 July. In August she was well enough to go hunting, staying on 19 August at Traquair House, home of the captain of her guard. Here she was joined by Darnley, but the royal pair were still estranged.

Later that month Prince James was taken to Stirling Castle, the traditional home of Scottish royal babies, and placed in the care of John Erskine, Earl of Mar, son of Mary's former guardian. Mary stayed with her son for several days and returned on 12 December for his christening, which took place on 17 December. The godparents were Elizabeth of England, who sent a gold font, Charles IX of France, Mary's brother-in-law, and her uncle, the Duke of Savoy. A torchlight procession brought the infant prince from the palace to the Chapel Royal, where he was christened James Charles. The ceremony was attended by many of the Scottish nobles, but not by the prince's father, who had now openly quarrelled with Mary.

The date 1566, part of the redecorations of 1615.

Opposite
The small room, or cabinet, off the queen's chamber in the royal palace in **Edinburgh Castle** where James VI was born. The ceiling and upper panelling date to 1615, when the room was restored in preparation of the visit of the king to the scene of his birth. This room, in its proportions, was typical of the private rooms of the nobility.

Traquair House was the home of Sir John Stewart, captain of the queen's bodyguard. Sir John was a second cousin to Mary and a strong supporter of the queen. Mary and Darnley visited Traquair on **19 August 1566** when trying to repair their failing marriage.

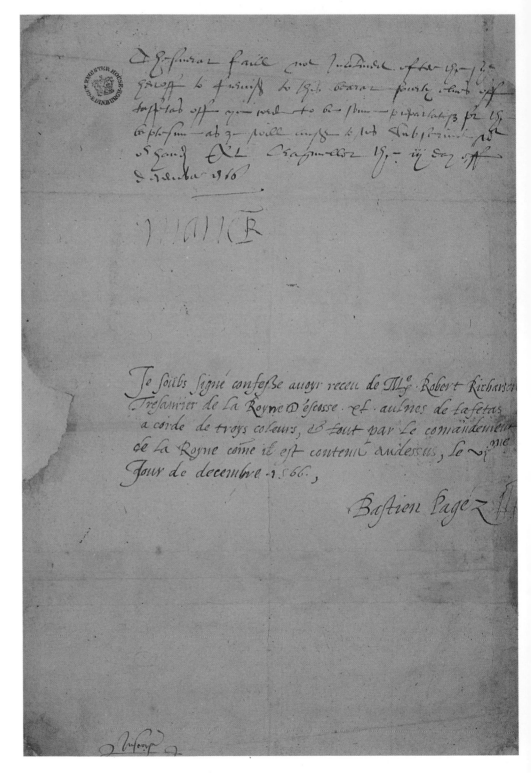

An authorisation from the queen to her treasurer to pay for and deliver to her servant, Bastien Pages, 40 ells of taffeta for the prince's forthcoming baptism. The order was made at Craigmillar Castle on 19 December 1566. It is receipted at the foot by Pages. Mary attended Pages' wedding masque at Holyroodhouse on the night that Darnley was murdered.

James VI as a child of about
six years, painted by Arnold
Bronckhorst.

John Erskine, Earl of Mar, guardian of James VI. From August
1565 to March 1567 Mar was keeper of Edinburgh Castle; in
that month he was appointed keeper of Stirling Castle. Mar
became Regent in 1571 following the murder of the Earl of
Lennox, but died in office the following year.

The royal palace in **Edinburgh
Castle**, probably established by
James III and considerably
extended by James IV. The
present fenestration dates to
the time of James VI; the
tower was heightened in the
nineteenth century. Mary lived
here from **3 April to 27 July
1566.**

The initials of Mary and Henry, with the date 1566, above
one of the doors of the palace. The doorway itself dates from
the seventeenth century and the panel bearing Mary and
Henry's monogram, so obviously an insert, may have been
taken from elsewhere (not necessarily in the castle) and placed
here during the refurbishing of the palace in preparation for
the homecoming of James VI in 1617.

MARY AND BOTHWELL

James Hepburn, 4th Earl of Bothwell. The earl was one of the most powerful Scottish lords.

'Upon the fifteenth day of May 1567, Mary, by the grace of God, Queen of Scots, was married on James, Duke of Orkney, Earl Bothwell . . . in the palace of Holyroodhouse . . . by Adam, Bishop of Orkney, not with the mass but with preaching, at ten hours afore noon.'

Diurnal of Occurrents in Scotland

THE BREACH between the Queen and the King of Scots was now public knowledge. In her predicament Mary turned for support to her nobles, and in particular to James Hepburn, Earl of Bothwell. The earl was one of the most powerful Border lords. He was Lord High Admiral of Scotland, Lord of Liddesdale, Crichton and Hailes, sheriff of Berwickshire, East and Mid Lothian and bailie of Lauderdale. In 1565 he had been given a special commission to enforce royal authority in the Borders. Like so many Scottish nobles, he was fickle in his relations with the Crown and in 1562 had actually spent some time imprisoned in Edinburgh Castle. On his escape he went into voluntary exile for three years before returning to Scotland in September 1565.

On 10 October 1566 Mary set out on her annual progress. This time the area chosen lay in the east Borders. She went first to Jedburgh, attending to the administration of justice. Sometime after Mary left Edinburgh she heard that Bothwell had been injured on 8 October in an affray with John Elliott of the Park. Mary continued presiding over her court of justice for several days until 16 October when she rode over to consult with Bothwell, now recuperating in his castle at Hermitage. The journey to and from Hermitage was over 80 km (50 miles), and it was accom-

Opposite

Hermitage Castle, the strength of Liddesdale, today gives the superficial appearance of dating to one period. In fact the castle expanded from a tower house, built in the late fourteenth century, over the fifteenth and sixteenth centuries to its present form. The corbelled parapet, which provides the misleading appearance of unity of design, was added in the nineteenth century. Hermitage was given to Patrick Hepburn, 1st Earl of Bothwell, by James IV in 1491. Apart from the years immediately following 1540, when Hermitage was seized by the Crown following treacherous negotiations between the Hepburns and the English king, the castle stayed in the hands of this family until the forfeiture of Francis Stewart, Earl of Bothwell, in 1593. Mary visited her wounded lieutenant, Bothwell, here on **16 October 1566.**

Crichton Castle grew in the later Middle Ages into a strong and compact courtyard castle. Throughout, it presented a grim face to the outside world, with few windows piercing the exterior wall. The castle was granted to Patrick Hepburn, Lord Hailes, in 1488 when he was created Earl of Bothwell. Mary came here on **10 to 12 January 1562** for the wedding of her half-brother, Lord James Stewart, to Lady Janet Hepburn. The son of that marriage, Francis Stewart, Earl of Bothwell, held the castle until his forfeiture in 1593.

Far right
Map indicating the route taken by Mary Queen of Scots and her entourage in 1566.

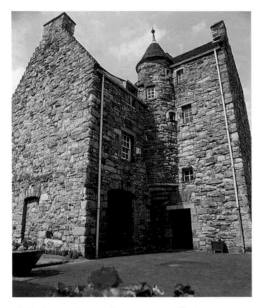

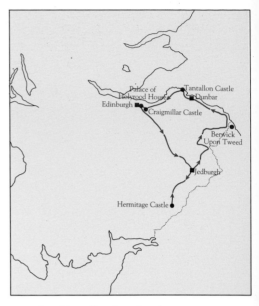

Mary is traditionally said to have stayed in this house, 'Queen Mary's House' (right), while residing in Jedburgh. In fact, the building may not have been erected until the reign of her son. Nevertheless, it remains an excellent example of a superior town house of the period, strongly built for defence. A small cannon (above), presented to Sir Thomas Kerr of Ferniehirst by Mary, and bearing the arms of France and Scotland, is preserved in the house.

plished in a day as there was insufficient accommodation in the castle for the queen, the Earl of Moray (now returned from England), her advisers and the soldiers forming her bodyguard.

On her return to Jedburgh the queen fell seriously ill. She probably suffered an attack of porphyria, a malady which she may have inherited from her father and which her son also suffered: this was the cause of the 'madness' of her descendant, George III. Before entering Edinburgh in November, Mary paused for some days at Craigmillar Castle. Here she discussed the problem of Darnley with her advisers. At first divorce was proposed, then

several nobles offered to do whatever was necessary to help the queen out of her predicament. The bond signed by, amongst others, the Earls of Argyll, Bothwell and Huntly led directly to the murder of Darnley at Kirk o'Field, beside the Edinburgh town walls, in the early hours of the morning of 10 February 1567.

Mary, it seems, was innocent of prior knowledge of the murder, but this was not generally believed by her fellow countrymen, especially as she was seen to rely increasingly on Bothwell, the man popularly believed to have murdered Darnley. The earl, in his turn, saw his opportunity. On

Craigmillar Castle was owned by Sir Simon Preston, a staunch supporter of Mary and a member of her Privy Council. The tower, rising high above the castle walls, was built by an ancestor of Sir Simon 100 years before. Following the English invasion of 1544, the curtain wall was repaired, and a new wall protecting the outer court built. Mary stayed here from **1 to 7 September 1563**, recuperating after her long tour of south-west Scotland. She returned to Craigmillar three years later, residing there from **20 November to 7 December 1566.** During that visit the plot was hatched to murder Darnley.

Far left
Burleigh Castle was the
inheritance of Margaret, wife
of Sir James Balfour, one of
the group which signed the
bond to murder Darnley. Like
so many Scottish castles of the
time, it consists of a tower
house (left), built here about
1500, with an attached
courtyard. In 1582 Balfour
rebuilt the courtyard wall,
adding the tower in the
foreground, which bears the
initials of himself and his wife
and the date. Sir James was
one of the murderers of
Cardinal Beaton in 1546 and,
following the capture of St
Andrews Castle, he served in
the galleys with John Knox. In
1567 he held Edinburgh Castle
for Mary and Bothwell, but for
a time he wavered, joining
Moray's party until the
Regent's death in 1570, when
he returned to his earlier
allegiance.

24 April he abducted the queen, as she was returning to Edinburgh from visiting her son at Stirling, and took her to Dunbar Castle. On 3 May he divorced his wife and on 15 May Mary and Bothwell were married at Holyroodhouse.

Even before the marriage the other Scottish nobles had been against Bothwell. As their strength grew, the queen and her consort left Edinburgh, moving into Bothwell's territory. Here they collected their forces and moved back towards Edinburgh. On 15 June 1567 the queen's army met that of the Scottish lords at Carberry, east of Edinburgh, and after a day of parleying the queen surrendered herself to the lords, and Bothwell returned to Dunbar. Mary was taken to Edinburgh and the following day consigned to Lochleven Castle, where she was to remain a prisoner for nearly a year. Bothwell tried to rally support for the queen. He moved north into Gordon country, but failed to persuade the Earl of Huntly to fight. He paused at Spynie Palace with his relative the bishop, but soon retreated to Orkney, of which he was duke and where he hoped to raise an army. Eventually he was forced to flee the country. He travelled to Norway where he was imprisoned for an earlier misdemeanour; he died in a Danish prison on 14 April 1578.

The Bishop's Palace in
Kirkwall, capital of Orkney,
was the seat of Bishop Adam
Bothwell who officiated at
Mary's third marriage. The
tower seen here was built by
his predecessor, Bishop Robert
Reid (1541–58).

Hailes Castle in East Lothian
was held by the Hepburns from
the fourteenth century. The
eastern part of the curtain wall
(to the left) dates to the
previous century, but the
ruined west tower (right) was
built by the Hepburns. The
castle changed hands several
times during the English raids
of the 1540s. Mary stopped
here on **5 May 1567**, while
travelling from Dunbar to
Edinburgh with Bothwell.

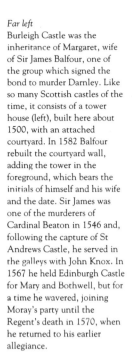

IMPRISONMENT AND ESCAPE

'Guard was continually kept at the castle day and night, except during supper, at which time the gate was locked with a key, every one going to supper, and the key was always placed on the table where the Governor took his meals, and before him.'

Giovanni Correr, Venetian ambassador to France, 26 May 1568

LOCHLEVEN CASTLE was a most suitable place for the rebellious Scottish lords to lodge the queen. Firstly, it was situated on an island, and thus escape was difficult. In fact, it had served as a prison on several occasions in the past, though then it had been the king who was locking up a rebellious subject. The advantage of its location was increased by its jailer, Sir William Douglas, half-brother to the Earl of Moray, now one of the leaders of the rebellious lords, and cousin to the Earl of Morton, the head of the Douglas family and another rebel.

The queen was lodged at first in one of the buildings in the courtyard, but a month later she was moved into the tower. Here she was assigned the third floor, which was divided into two rooms. These rooms seem small, but they were no smaller than most of the private rooms of the nobility, and they are those which Mary would have occupied on her previous visits to the castle. However, on this occasion no rich furnishings accompanied the queen as they had before; the contrast between the present and the past must have been marked. Mary was even kept short of clothes and repeatedly demanded that dresses, cloth and threads be sent to her from Holyroodhouse, though rarely with success.

Mary was not allowed privacy in this room for usually Lady Douglas also slept in it, in order to keep a close watch on the prisoner. However, an advantage for Mary was that the embrasure of the east window had earlier been modified to serve as a place for prayer. An altar shelf had been inserted with a *piscina* (basin) and a small wall cupboard.

Mary is known to have spent much time in needlework while at Lochleven Castle. She was allowed to walk in the grounds of the castle but

The fourteenth-century tower was Mary's prison in **Lochleven Castle**. Her quarters lay on the third floor, where she was confined to two rooms. Mary was not even allowed the privacy of her own bedroom for she frequently had to share it with Lady Douglas.

Opposite
Lochleven Castle viewed across the waters of the loch. This was no strange prison for Mary as she had visited the castle on several occasions previously. Lochleven was a convenient stopping-place while journeying through Fife. The queen was related to the Douglases of Lochleven. In **April 1563**, while staying at the castle, the queen had sent for John Knox, one of the Protestant leaders, to discuss religious and state affairs. On **9 September 1565** Mary and Darnley had stopped for dinner here while on their honeymoon.

The tower and courtyard of **Lochleven Castle**. Mary may at first have been lodged in the ruined building in the foreground.

these walks were circumscribed by the size of the island which in the sixteenth century extended little beyond the castle walls, the water of the loch being higher than today.

A little over a month after her arrival at Lochleven Castle, Mary miscarried of twins and then, while she was recovering, she was forced to abdicate in favour of her infant son on 24 July 1567. One of those who forced the abdication on Mary was William, Lord Ruthven, son of Patrick Ruthven who had led the party which murdered Riccio. Now, depressed, isolated and in fear of her life, Mary waited rescue.

The first attempt at escape failed, but on 2 May 1568, with the aid of George and Willie Douglas, Mary escaped across the loch to be met by her supporters. Mary crossed the Forth at Queensferry

The Abdication of Mary, by Gavin Hamilton (1723–98). This romantic impression shows Mary signing the deed of abdication in Lochleven Castle watched by Patrick, Lord Lindsay, William, Lord Ruthven, and Sir William Douglas of Lochleven.

Craignethan Castle was built in the 1530s by Sir James Hamilton of Finnart, illegitimate son of the 1st Earl of Arran and thus a kinsman of James V. Sir James was also employed by the king to supervise the remodelling of Falkland Palace. Craignethan utilised all the most up-to-date methods of defence. After Sir James' execution in 1540, Craignethan was acquired by his half-brother, James Hamilton, later Duke of Châtelherault. The castle was seized by Regent Moray following Mary's defeat at Langside, but it was soon recaptured by Lord Claud Hamilton, and served as one of the main bases of Mary's supporters until 1573. The insane 3rd Earl of Arran, Châtelherault's son, lived in the castle from 1575 to 1579; in 1561 he had been a suitor for Mary's hand.

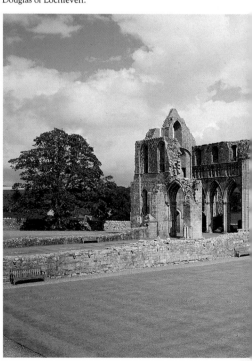

and rode first to Niddry Castle. Here she gave instructions for the raising of her adherents and moved rapidly on to Cadzow, the chief seat of the Hamiltons, near the modern town of Hamilton. For several days she remained on the move between Cadzow, where she stayed at night, and another Hamilton castle in the vicinity, Craignethan. Supporters flocked to her cause, but when the queen's army gave battle at Langside on 13 May, her larger army was defeated by the better-led force of her half-brother, Moray.

Mary now fled southwards, staying each night at the house of a friend, until on 15 May she arrived at the Abbey of Dundrennan on the north shore of the Solway Firth. She had already made the fateful decision to cross into England and appeal to her cousin, Elizabeth, for help, and on 16 May she sailed across the Solway to Workington.

Map indicating Mary's route from Lochleven Castle to Langside and thence to Carlisle.

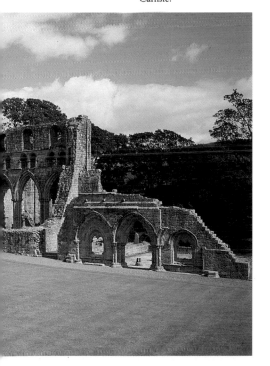

Left
Niddry Castle, Winchburgh, where Mary paused on **2 May 1568** to summon her forces before proceeding on to Cadzow Castle, stronghold of the Duke of Châtelherault. Niddry Castle is open to the public only by appointment.

Centre
Dundrennan Abbey was founded by David I in 1142 for the Cistercians. Today the only parts of the church to survive to full height are the transepts and side walls of the presbytery, built in the late twelfth century at the time of transition from Romanesque to Gothic architecture. Mary spent the night of **15 May 1568** here, her last night on Scottish soil.

EXILE

'I am in a walled enclosure, on top of a hill, exposed to all the winds and inclemencies of heaven.'

Mary Queen of Scots, Tutbury Castle, 1584

MARY LANDED at Workington after a few hours crossing and was taken to Carlisle Castle, where she spent two months before being moved south to Bolton Castle in Yorkshire. She came to England with the intention of appealing to her cousin, Queen Elizabeth, for aid against the rebellious Scottish lords. It was to be some time before the realities of her situation became apparent, and her intended brief exile turned into a long imprisonment, which ended on the scaffold 19 years later.

In the meantime, in Scotland, loyal nobles rallied to the queen's cause. While Mary's half-brother, the Earl of Moray, was Regent for the infant James VI, he certainly did not control the whole country. The Hamiltons remained loyal to the queen and several royal castles held out for her. While attempting to extend his control over the whole country, Moray was assassinated on 23 January 1570 at Linlithgow by a member of the Hamilton family.

Carlisle Castle was the principal English stronghold in the West Marches. The twelfth-century keep rises above the 6 m high curtain wall and ditch. Mary was here from **19 May to 15 July 1568.**

Opposite
This tower in Carlisle Castle is popularly known as Queen Mary's Tower. Dating to the fourteenth century, it is one of the few buildings to have survived from Mary's time. It served as the stair tower of the eastern gatehouse, which was rebuilt in the nineteenth century.

South Wingfield Manor, built in the fifteenth century, lies between Derby and Sheffield. Mary first came here on **20 April 1569.** She moved on to Chatsworth on **15 May,** but returned on **1 June,** staying until **21 September.** She returned to Wingfield from **August to November 1584.** Wingfield was one of the several houses owned by the Earl of Shrewsbury, Mary's custodian from 1569 until 1584.

The queen's forced abdication and flight into England split Scotland into two armed camps. The civil war was brought to an end by the Pacification of Perth, signed on 23 February 1573, and the fall of Edinburgh Castle on 29 May 1573. Many monuments associated with both sides in this civil war are in the care of Historic Buildings and Monuments. Those which appear on these pages—Queen's Party to the left, King's Party to the right—have not appeared elsewhere in this book.

Carnasserie Castle in Argyll, seat of John Carswell, Bishop of the Isles.

Duffus Castle in Moray, home of Alexander Sutherland.

Robert Crichton, Bishop of Dunkeld, inclined to the Queen's Party.

Crossraguel Abbey in Ayrshire. Alan Stewart, Commendator (lay administrator) of Crossraguel, supported the queen.

The Commendator of Ardchattan in Argyll was a Campbell and probably followed the head of his family, the Earl of Argyll, into the Queen's Party.

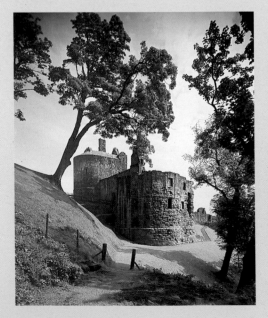

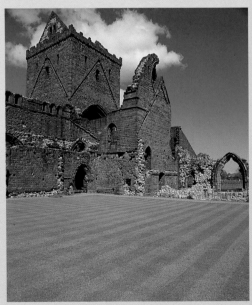

Ravenscraig Castle in Fife, property of William, 4th Lord Sinclair, who died in 1570.

Far right
Gilbert Brown, Commendator of Sweetheart Abbey near Dumfries, was a queen's man.

The Commendator of Cambuskenneth, near Stirling, was an Erskine and followed the head of his family, the Earl of Mar, into the King's Party.

Mar's Wark in Stirling, built in 1570 by the Earl of Mar during his regency, but unfinished at his death.

Tullibardine Chapel, near Auchterarder, founded by Sir David Murray in 1446. Sir William Murray of Tullibardine was Comptroller of the Queen's Household, but joined the King's Party.

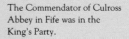

Robert Keith, Commendator of Deer Abbey in Aberdeenshire, was probably a member of the King's Party, as was the head of his family, the Earl Marischal.

The Commendator of Culross Abbey in Fife was in the King's Party.

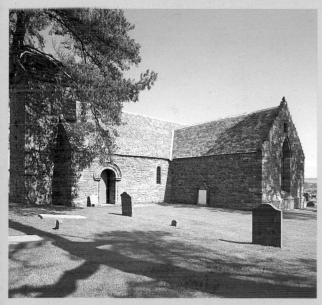

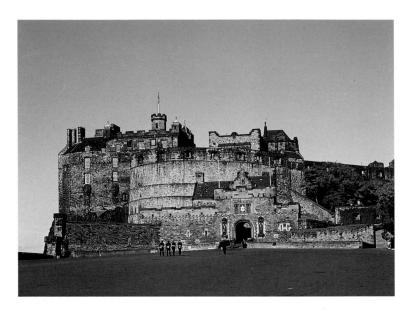

Moray's successor as Regent was the Earl of Lennox, Darnley's father. He in turn, was killed in a skirmish at Stirling in September 1571 to be succeeded by the Earl of Mar. Mar died naturally in his bed a year later, and his successor, the Earl of Morton, was Regent until 1578: in 1581 he was executed for his part in Darnley's murder. During his six years as Regent, Morton brought the civil war in Scotland to an end. Doune Castle was captured in 1570 and Dumbarton Castle in 1571; Blackness fell in February 1573. Finally, in May 1573, Edinburgh Castle was captured, its defender Kirkcaldy of Grange executed, and the queen's cause in Scotland effectively dead.

Edinburgh Castle from the Esplanade. The castle was held for Mary from her exile in 1568 until May 1573. The leaders of the defence were Sir William Kirkcaldy of Grange and William Maitland of Lethington, formerly the queen's Secretary of State. Kirkcaldy was one of the foremost Scottish soldiers of the day, and had led the forces opposed to Mary at Langside. The siege was brought to an end through the use of cannon lent by Elizabeth I. The main east front, devastated by cannonfire, was entirely rebuilt. The Portcullis Gate and the Half Moon Battery, both the work of Regent Morton, date to these years. The latter served as an emplacement for artillery which would protect the gentle east approach to the castle.

The memorial to Sir William Kirkcaldy of Grange in Edinburgh Castle. This records his defence of the castle in the queen's cause from May 1568 to May 1573.

The fighting between the queen's supporters and her enemies extended over much of Scotland. In the north-east the Gordon Earls of Huntly were loyal until February 1573 when they came to terms with Regent Morton. In November 1571 Adam Gordon of Auchindoun (see page 47) attacked Corgarff Castle and when Margaret Forbes, wife of the laird, refused to surrender, he set it on fire; Margaret Forbes, her family and servants, about 24 in number, perished. Corgarff was remodelled after the 1745 rebellion, the curtain wall being built then. The tower, originally constructed in the middle of the sixteenth century, is where the events of 1571 occurred.

Blackness Castle on the Firth of Forth, built in the 1440s, passed into the hands of the Crown in 1453 and has been a royal castle since that date, remaining in use as an army installation until 1912. The castle was strengthened by James V, then repaired following a siege in 1650; subsequent additions have mostly been removed. The appearance of the castle today is thus not very different from that in Mary's reign. From 1543 to 1548 the Duke of Châtelherault, Regent for the infant queen, used Blackness Castle as a stronghold for himself and a residence for his children, but from 1548 until 1560 it was garrisoned by the French. In that year a Hamilton was appointed governor, remaining until 1567. The castle was secured for the Queen's Party on 21 February 1572 by Lord Claud Hamilton. Its garrison harried shipping on the Forth and attacked the Fife burghs. The castle was recaptured by the King's Party on 10 February 1573 through a combination of treachery and intrigue.

Slezer's view of **Dumbarton Castle** from the north-west was drawn about 1690; the castle was probably little altered from Mary's time. Its governor, Lord Fleming, had accompanied Mary to England, but returned to Dumbarton and successfully defended the castle against Regent Moray in 1570. The siege was raised after Moray's murder, but renewed the following year, when it fell to Captain Crawford on 1 April. Crawford and his men ascended the near precipitous north-east slopes and surprised and overpowered the defenders. Lord Fleming escaped, but John Hamilton, Archbishop of St Andrews, brother of the Duke of Châtelherault, was captured and executed.

Two of these fragments of embroidery, originally part of a single panel, are the work of Mary while in exile, and are now in the **Palace of Holyroodhouse**. One of the pieces depicts a ginger cat playing with a mouse, an allusion to Mary's own position (Queen Elizabeth had red hair). The second bears the monogram M and F, for Mary and Francis. The third was the work of Bess of Hardwick, Countess of Shrewsbury, the wife of Mary's jailer. These fragments form part of a series of panels, most of which are now displayed in Oxburgh Hall, Norfolk.

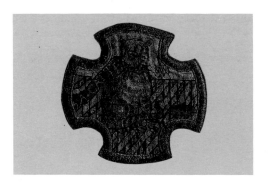

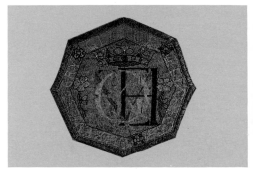

Mary herself was to live for another 14 years. She had been moved south from Bolton Castle early in 1569 and she spent the remaining years of her life at a succession of castles and houses in the middle of England, strategically placed as far away from both Scotland and London as practicable. Here she turned increasingly to needlework, and to plotting. Plotting was to be her undoing, and, after the uncovering of the Babington Plot in 1586, she was executed at Fotheringhay Castle on 8 February 1587.

The effigy of Mary Queen of Scots on her tomb in Westminster Abbey. In 1612 James VI brought his mother's body here from Peterborough Cathedral where she had been buried in 1587. He also ordered the demolition of Fotheringhay Castle, the scene of her execution.

FURTHER READING

There are innumerable books on Mary Queen of Scots. The following serve as an introduction:

J K Cheetham, *Mary Queen of Scots, the Captive Years*, Sheffield 1982.
I Cowan, *The Enigma of Mary Queen of Scots*, London 1971.

G Donaldson, *Mary Queen of Scots*, London 1974.
G Donaldson, *All the Queen's Men*, London 1983.
A Fraser, *Mary Queen of Scots*, London 1969.
R K Marshall, *Queen of Scots*, Edinburgh 1986.
A Plowden, *Two Queens in One Isle*, London 1985.
M Swain, *The Needlework of Mary Queen of Scots*, reprinted 1986.

ACKNOWLEDGEMENTS

Much new photography for this book has been undertaken by Mr David Henrie. The illustrations on the following pages are reproduced by gracious permission of Her Majesty the Queen: 8 (Charles IX, Edward VI and Mary); 13 (Don Carlos); 14; 27 (arms); 30; 31 (ceiling); 32 (ceiling); 33; 34 (pomander); 53 (Darnley) and 78 (embroidery). Other illustrations are reproduced by kind permission of: Airviews (M/r) Ltd, 13 (Berwick upon Tweed); Major David Baxter, 55 (Earlshall); Courtauld Institute of Art, 8 (Francis II and Henry II); The Fine Art Society plc, front cover; A Forbes, inside front cover and 2; French Government Tourist Office, 26 and 27 (Chambord); Duke of Hamilton, 10 (Châtelherault); Historic Buildings and Monuments Commission, England, 72 and 73; Hunterian Art Gallery, University of Glasgow, 70 (*Abdication*); Earl of Moray, 11 (Moray); National Gallery of Scotland, 58; National Library of Scotland, 52; National Portrait Gallery, England, 8 (Elizabeth I, Henry VIII and Philip II), 9 (Edward VI), 13 (Leicester) and 15 (Elizabeth I); National Museums of Scotland, 10 (coin), 22, 34 (cabinet and hanging), 43 (coin) and 55 (coin); National Trust, 8 (Francis II); National Trust for Scotland, 36, 37 (Falkland); Public Record Office, England, 15 (Carberry); Sir David Ogilvy, 52; Scottish National Portrait Gallery, 4, 7, 8 (Bothwell, Darnley, James V, James VI and Mary of Guise), 15 (Bothwell and his wife), 35 (John Knox), 41 (Seton), 43 (Morton), 63 (James VI and Mar), 65 (Bothwell); Scottish Record Office, 62; Scottish Tourist Board, 46 (Dunnottar) and 61 (Traquair); Society of Antiquaries of London, 8 (Mary Tudor); Trustees of the Victoria and Albert Museum, 73 (Mary) and the Dean and Chapter of Westminster Abbey, 78 (tomb). We are also grateful to the following for assistance with photography at their properties: Duke of Hamilton (Lennoxlove); Earl of Mansfield (Scone Palace); Earl of Strathmore (Glamis Castle); National Trust for Scotland (Balmerino Abbey and Falkland Palace) and Roxburgh District Museums ('Queen Mary's House'). The maps and the plan of the queen's apartments at Holyroodhouse were prepared by Mr T Borthwick. Grateful thanks are also due to Mr C J Burnett, Dr E Furgol, Mrs J Henrie, Dr R K Marshall, Miss H E Smailes, Mrs M Swain, Lt Col D J C Wickes and colleagues in Historic Buildings and Monuments for help in the preparation of this book.

Miniature of Mary by Nicholas Hilliard, painted about 1578.

Sites in heavy type are in the care of Historic Buildings and Monuments and open to the public (Inverlochy Castle, Lochmaben Castle and Spynie Palace may be viewed from the outside only).

Reference to pages with illustrations are given in italics after text references.

Printed in Scotland for HMSO by Holmes McDougall Ltd 1/87. D'd 287006